# The World And Its Arse

David Muncaster

www.silvermonpublishing.co.uk

© 2014 David Muncaster

A Division of Silvermoon Productions Limited
3rd Floor | 207 Regent Street | London | W1B 3HH
0207 0961603
www.silvermoonpublishing.co.uk

ISBN 978-1-910457-04-7

Silvermoon Publishing is an innovative publishing house established to publish plays and license rights to theatre companies world-wide. Silvermoon aims to promote its plays and playwrights to ensure that its playwrights get maximum exposure.

Rights of performance for Silvermoon plays are controlled by Silvermoon Publishing, 3rd Floor, 207 Regent Street, London W1B 3HH who will issue a performing licence on payment of a fee and subject to a number of conditions. These plays are fully protected under the Copyright Laws of the British Commonwealth of Nations, the United States of America and all countries of the Berne and Universal Copyright Conventions. All rights, including stage, motion picture, radio, television, public reading and translation into foreign languages are strictly reserved. It is an infringement of the copyright to give any performance or public reading of these plays before the fee has been paid and the licence issued. The royalty fee is subject to contract and subject to variation at the sole discretion of Silvermoon Publishing. In territories overseas the fees quoted in this catalogue may not apply. A fee will be quoted on application to Silvermoon Publishing.

The right of David Muncaster to be identified as author of this work has been asserted by him in accordance with Section 77 of the Copyright, Designs and Patents Act 1988

### COPYRIGHT INFORMATION

The play is fully protected under the Copyright laws of the British Commonwealth of Nations, the United States of America and all countries of the Berne and Universal Copyright Conventions.

All rights including Stage, Motion Picture, Radio, television, Public Reading, and Translation into Foreign Languages, are strictly reserved.

No part of this publication may lawfully be reproduced in ANY form or by any means - photocopying, typescript, recording (including video-recording), manuscript, electronic, mechanical or otherwise - or be transmitted or stored in a retrieval system, without prior permission.

Licenses for amateur performances are issued subject to the understanding that it shall be made clear in all advertising matter that the audience will witness an amateur performance; that the names of the authors of the plays shall be included on all programmes, and that the integrity of the authors' work will be preserved.

The Royalty Fee is subject to contract and subject to variation at the sole discretion of Silvermoon Publishing.

In Theatres of Halls seating Four Hundred or more the fee will be subject to negotiation.

In Territories Overseas the fee quoted may not apply. A fee will be quoted on application to Silvermoon Publishing, London.

## VIDEO-RECORDING OF AMATEUR PRODUCTIONS

Please note that the copyright laws governing video-recording are extremely complex and that it should not be assumed that any play may be video-recorded for whatever purpose without first obtaining the permission of the appropriate agents. The fact that a play is published by Silvermoon Publishing does not indicate that video rights are available or that Silvermoon Publishing control such rights.

## PERFORMING LICENCE APPLICATIONS

A performing licence for these plays will be issued by "Silvermoon Publishing" subject to the following conditions:-

1. That the performance fee is paid in full on the date of application for a licence.
2. That the name of the author(s) is/are clearly shown in any programme or publicity material.
3. That the author(s) is/are entitled to receive two complimentary tickets to see his/her/their work in performance if they so wish.
4. That a copy of the play is purchased from Silvermoon Publishing for each named speaking part and a minimum of three copies purchased for backstage use.
5. That a copy of any reviews / Marketing materials be forwarded to Silvermoon Publishing.
6. That the Silvermoon Publishing licensing statement be displayed on any marketing material.

## FEES

Details of script prices and fees payable for each performance or public reading can be obtained by telephone to (+44) 0207 0961603 or to the address below. Alternatively, latest prices can be obtained from our website. www.silvermoonpublishing.co.uk.

To apply for a performing licence for any play please write to Silvermoon Publishing, 3rd Floor, 207 Regent Street, London W1B 3HH or email via our website with the following details:-

1. Name and address of theatre company.
2. Details of venue including seating capacity.
3. Dates of proposed performance or public reading.
4. Contact telephone number for Author's complimentary tickets.

Or apply directly via our website at www.silvermoonpublishing.co.uk

## PROFESSIONAL RIGHTS

Professional rights for Nativity should be addressed to Silvermoon Publishing.

# DAVID MUNCASTER

Theatre has been part of David's life ever since his school days. He is on record for saying that drama studies were just about the only thing he was any good at, but turned down an opportunity to work at the Nottingham Playhouse as an Assistant Stage Manager because the cost of rent, food and bus fare were greater than the salary on offer. Instead he immersed himself into amateur theatre where he has done everything with the exception of prompt; which he wouldn't do "for all the tea in China"!

He began writing as a teenager, firstly lyrics for a rock band then articles for a student magazine before starting work on his first book. It took a surprising long time before David finally combined his passion for theatre with writing but his first play, Call Girls was an immediate success being published by New Theatre Publications and having performances in both the UK and the USA. Since then there have been hundreds of performances of David's work around the world by both amateur and professional companies with his festival friendly one act plays regularly winning awards.

In 2010 he answered an advertisement in Amateur Stage for a playscript reviewer and with an average of eight plays a month his reviews have become one of the most popular features in the magazine.

David lives in Cheshire where he is an active participant for two amateur groups and an enthusiastic supporter of all forms of theatre.

*www.davidmuncaster.com*

## CAST

**Frank** (Male, Eighties) Fidgets and talks to himself. Has Parkinson's Disease. Well Spoken.
**Nurse** (Female, Thirties) Friendly, stressed, professional.
**Porter** (Male, Forties) Uncompromisingly cheerful.
**Brian** (Male, Forties) Timid, put-upon.
**Doctor** (Male, Any age) Cold, busy.
**Sister** (Female, Any age) Cool, professional.
**Len** (Male, Seventies) Hardly conscious. Gentle.
**Judith** (Female, Forties) Brian's wife. Angry.
**Maureen** (Female, Seventies) Len's wife. Scared.
**Rosie** (Female, Forties) Len's daughter. Practical.
**John** (Male, Fifties) Frank's son. Menacing.
**Victoria** (Female, Teens) Brian's daughter. Astute.

## AUTHOR'S NOTE FOR THE WORLD AND ITS ARSE

This is probably the most personal play that I have written. I spent three weeks in a NHS hospital a few years ago, being shunted from one ward to the next and being sent for numerous tests without ever seeing the Lesser Spotted Urologist. The similarity with Brian ends right there but all the characters are based on real people that I encountered during my stay and if anyone recognises themselves I hope they realise that I remember them all with affection. Mostly, though, I hope that I have captured my admiration for the total professionalism displayed by all the staff who do a very difficult job under often impossible circumstances for very little reward. I am proud of the NHS but I am more proud of the people that it employs.

# ACT ONE

**SCENE ONE**

*A hospital ward. Three beds each with armchairs and cupboards. Curtains surround the centre bed. The bed to the right belongs to FRANK who is sitting in the armchair next to his bed. His speech is littered with pauses during which he fidgets or stares into space.*

**FRANK:** Can you hear them?
Buggers. Clear off!
They think I can't hear them. I know they're there. I know you're there.
Buggers.
Using my yard. Doing their drugs and what have you. Taking advantage. I'll put an end to it.
Yes me! Why not me? I can put an end to it.
Taking advantage. Yes you did. (*There are voices off.*)
Clear off. Do you hear me? Clear off. (*More voices.*)
I'll have the police on you.
Do you hear me?
I'll speak to the police.

**NURSE:** (*Off*) Frank.

**FRANK:** Little buggers. Leave me alone.

**NURSE:** (*Off*) Frank. I'll be with you in a minute.

**FRANK:** You must think I'm soft. Clear off. Using my yard. Trying to frighten me. They are. They're trying to frighten me. I'll give them something to think about. I can sort them out myself. I don't need any help. Don't need YOUR help.

Yes you! I'm talking to you. Don't look at your mother. What? What did you say? What?
That was a nasty trick you pulled. A nasty trick.

(*Becomes distressed. Sings.*)

Fairest Lord Jesus, Ruler of all nature, O Thou of God and man the Son, Thee will I cherish, Thee will I honour, Thou, my soul's glory, joy and crown. (*Tries to stand.*)
Someone's glued this. Would you believe it?
The buggers have glued this. That's a nasty trick. A nasty trick they pulled. It's all... I can't...

**NURSE:** (*Off*) I'll be with you next, Frank.

**FRANK:** Fuck off.

**NURSE:** (Off) That's not very nice.

**FRANK:** You just fuck...
I won't...
Don't you come in here. Now, do you hear me?

**NURSE:** (*Enters*) Now, stop that. I won't have it, Frank. I won't have you talking to me like that.

**FRANK:** Oh. Sorry.

**NURSE:** That's better.

**FRANK:** I'm ever so sorry.

**NURSE:** All right, Frank. Now be quiet a minute, I won't be long. (*Exits*) FRANK fidgets in his chair.

**FRANK:** Yes, you can laugh. Taking advantage. What! Who's bloody glued this? Oh bloody hell. (*Sings*)
Breathe on me, breath of God, Fill me with life anew...
Oh, bloody hell.
I've got to get away from here. Thieves the lot of them. I'm an old man. I've got nothing. What do they want to steal from me for? What good is it to them?
No. I can't stay here.
I'll tell her when she comes.
It's all right. You can go. Yes, yes. I'll be all right. Don't worry. No, no.
Ah! Look at this. The bloody buggers. They've glued all this. What do you want to do that for?
You should be ashamed of yourself. Stealing from an old man. Yes, you.
Come here boy. I'm talking to you.

**NURSE:** (*Enters*) Now then, Frank. I'm all yours.

**FRANK:** Eh?

**NURSE:** You pressed your buzzer. Don't you remember?

**FRANK:** Buzzer?

**NURSE:** You pressed your call button. Did you want something?

**FRANK:** Yes, I do. I do want something.

**NURSE:** Well, are you going to tell me or shall we play twenty questions?

**FRANK:** I'll tell you, yes, I'll tell you.

**NURSE:** Good. Go on then, Frank.

**FRANK:** I want my, my thing back.

**NURSE:** Your thing? Give us a clue then, mate. What thing?

**FRANK:** They're all bloody thieves round here. You can't leave anything. Someone will have it.

**NURSE:** What thing?

**FRANK:** Bloody buggers, they are.

**NURSE:** Who are?

**FRANK:** Them. All of them.

**NURSE:** You are going to need to be a bit more specific, mate.

**FRANK:** Eh?

**NURSE:** What have you lost, Frank?

**FRANK:** I haven't lost anything.

**NURSE:** No? Silly me. I thought you just said you had.

**FRANK:** It's been stolen.

**NURSE:** What's been stolen?

**FRANK:** That thing there. That frame. That's mine.

**NURSE:** The Zimmer frame? That's not yours, Frank.

**FRANK:** Yes, that.
He...
He's stolen it.

**NURSE:** Who's stolen it? Len? Len hasn't stolen it, it belongs to him.

**FRANK:** It's mine that is. He doesn't need it. He's got one.

**NURSE:** Yes, he has got one. That's it.

**FRANK:** It's mine.

**NURSE:** It isn't, Frank.

**FRANK:** What does he want to steal it for?

**NURSE:** Frank. Frank, listen to me. That is Len's frame. You don't have a frame. You don't need one.

**FRANK:** Len?

**NURSE:** Yes, Frank. It belongs to Len.

**FRANK:** Len?

**NURSE:** Yes. Len in the next bed.

**FRANK:** It belongs to Len?

**NURSE:** Yes. You don't need a frame. You can walk without one.

**FRANK:** Oh.

**NURSE:** That's right.

**FRANK:** Oh, I'm sorry.

**NURSE:** That's OK.

**FRANK:** I hope I haven't caused any trouble.

**NURSE:** No.

| | |
|---|---|
| **FRANK:** | I don't want to offend anyone. |
| **NURSE:** | Yes, well. Stop it with the swearing, that might help. |
| **FRANK:** | Eh? Swearing? Who's swearing? |
| **NURSE:** | Never mind, Frank. Do you want anything else while I'm here? Pedicure? Leg wax? |
| **FRANK:** | Eh? |
| **NURSE:** | See you later, Frank. |
| | (*Nurse Exits*) FRANK fidgets. |
| **FRANK:** | Taking advantage. Yes, you. I'm talking to you. Don't look at your mother, she can't help you. That was a nasty trick you pulled. (*He fidgets.*) <br> Forty thousand pounds. It's a bloody joke. You're not leaving it like that. You can't leave it like that. Cowboys! Well you are. <br> What the... Who's glued all this? |

*PORTER enters pushing BRIAN in a wheelchair. He stops at the bed next to the window.*

| | |
|---|---|
| **PORTER:** | Here we are. Ground floor: perfumery, stationery and leather goods, wigs and haberdashery, kitchenware and food. Going up! |

*BRIAN is dressed in pyjamas and a dressing gown. He stands and puts the bag that had been on his lap on to the bed.*

| | |
|---|---|
| **BRIAN:** | I told them, I could have walked. |
| **PORTER:** | Can't have that. The goblins would be up in arms. |
| **BRIAN:** | Goblins? |
| **PORTER:** | Elf and safety. |
| **BRIAN:** | Oh, I see. |
| **PORTER:** | You got everything you need? |

**BRIAN:** I think so.

**PORTER:** You haven't left anything on the other ward? Ipod?

**BRIAN:** Got it here.

**PORTER:** Louis Vuitton handbag? GHD straightener? Wonderbra?

**BRIAN:** Only at weekends.

**PORTER:** Set of encyclopedias?

**BRIAN:** I've decided to leave them behind for the other patients.

**PORTER:** How noble of you. Laptop? Mobile?

**BRIAN:** In the bag.

**PORTER:** Not that you are allowed to use your mobile of course.

**BRIAN:** Well... I mean. I go into the TV room to use it, of course.

**PORTER:** Don't worry. Nurses are on theirs all the time. I didn't tell you that, though.

**BRIAN:** Oh, right.

**PORTER:** Make yourself comfortable. Nurse will be along in a minute. (*PORTER addresses FRANK.*) You all right there Frank?

**FRANK:** Eh?

**PORTER:** You all right?

**FRANK:** I'm all right.

**PORTER:** Tell you what, Frank. I had a bit of a mishap on Ward 7, mate. This guy is on a life support machine...

**FRANK:** Life support?

**PORTER:** Yeah, and I'm walking by and he shouts to me so I go over and he says 'turn it off.' I says 'no I can't' but he says, 'please, please just turn it off' and I says 'it isn't that bad is it?' and he says 'yes, just turn it off', I says 'I can't' and he says 'I can't do it myself, please do it for me' and I look into his sad, pleading eyes and I can't stand it any more so I do it, I turn off his life support. I know I shouldn't but I could see him suffer so I stand there watching him for a minute, see the life draining from his face and I can't bear to look so I turn around. That's when I noticed the telly.

**FRANK:** Telly?

**PORTER:** Yeah. The telly.

*PORTER starts to laugh. FRANK smiles and then begins to laugh himself. We are not sure whether he has actually understood the joke.*

**PORTER:** Here let me make you a bit more comfortable.

*PORTER adjusts FRANK's blanket etc. BRIAN peers round the curtained bed to address FRANK.*

**BRIAN:** Hello there.

**FRANK:** Eh?

**BRIAN:** I'm Brian.

**FRANK:** Brian?

**BRIAN:** Yes.

**FRANK:** You're not Brian.

**PORTER:** You tell him, Frank.

*NURSE enters.*

**NURSE:** Mr Taylor?

**BRIAN:** Yes.

**NURSE:** I'm Kim. You've come from Ward Six, I believe.

**BRIAN:** Yes, third ward I've been in this week.

**NURSE:** Yes, it's always a struggle for beds. Look, I'll come and get you sorted in a bit. There's one or two things I have to do. Just make yourself comfortable.

*As NURSE exits she addresses PORTER.*

**NURSE:** Thanks, Porter. Next time check in with me please.

**PORTER:** Whatever you say, Nurse Kim. (*He winks at BRIAN.*) See you later, Frank. Take care, mate.

*PORTER exits. BRIAN produces an iPod, plugs in his earpiece and lies on his bed.*

**NURSE:** (*Off*) Oh, Dr Samuel, could I just...

*DOCTOR enters and goes behind the curtain of the centre bed.*

**DOCTOR:** Mr Wilson. I'm Doctor Samuel. How are you feeling? Mr Wilson, where is your cannula? Oh, really.

*DOCTOR exits. Voices off, then DOCTOR returns with SISTER. They go behind the curtain.*

**DOCTOR:** It's not good enough.

**SISTER:** He must have pulled it out.

**DOCTOR:** Of course he pulled it out, but why didn't anyone notice?

**SISTER:** It's a bit difficult with the curtain around him.

**DOCTOR:** Yes but why has he got the curtain round him?

**SISTER:** I thought you had requested it.

**DOCTOR:** Me?

**SISTER:** Didn't you?

**DOCTOR:** Why would I want you to curtain off my patient?

**SISTER:** Don't ask me, Doctor.

*SISTER draws the curtain back to reveal LEN who is apparently sleeping. DOCTOR's pager bleeps.*

**DOCTOR:** Get a cannula on him, he needs saline.

*DOCTOR exits.*

**SISTER:** Yes, Dr Samuel.

*SISTER exits.*

**FRANK:** They've glued it all up. All round here. Buggers.

*BRIAN removes his earplugs.*

**BRIAN:** Did you say something?

**FRANK:** Eh?

**BRIAN:** Did you speak?

**FRANK:** I spoke. Yes I spoke.

**BRIAN:** Right. I've come up from Ward Six. Ward Eleven before that. Waiting to see a Urologist. They seem to be a bit of a rare species. Been here a week and haven't spotted one yet. By the time I get to see one I won't have whatever it was that I came in with. I'm not even sure I've got it now. Whatever it is. Have you been in long?

**FRANK:** Too long.

**BRIAN:** Well, any time in hospital is too long isn't it?

**FRANK:** Not when you're old.

**BRIAN:** You like it then?

**FRANK:** Eh?

**BRIAN:** You don't mind being here.

**FRANK:** Here?

**BRIAN:** Yes.

**FRANK:** I'm here. Yes.

**BRIAN:** Right.

**FRANK:** I was always very active, you know.

**BRIAN:** Oh, really.

**FRANK:** English and P.E. Funny combination. People used to say.

**BRIAN:** You were a teacher?

**FRANK:** Healthy minds and healthy bodies you see.

**BRIAN:** Can't be bad.

**FRANK:** Give them a proper start.

**BRIAN:** Not like that now eh? Don't even teach them grammar any more. When I see some of the stuff my Vicky hands in, doesn't even make sense, but her teachers seem happy enough with it. Pages upon pages without any punctuation. How can anyone read that?

**FRANK:** I know you, don't I?

**BRIAN:** I don't think so.

**FRANK:** You were one of my lads.

**BRIAN:** At your school you mean? No. I'm not from round here. I moved with work.

**FRANK:** Yes. I remember you. Always were cheeky.
Back of the classroom. Hiding behind the lid of your desk.
Smirking. Passing notes around.

**BRIAN:** You're thinking of someone else.

**FRANK:** I knew you wouldn't amount to much.
Call that a conservatory? It's a bloody state.
Try to cheat an old man would you?
How much? That's more than I paid for the house.
Bloody buggers.

*NURSE enters and closes the curtains around LEN staying on the inside.*

**NURSE:** Right, Len. Going to put a new cannula in. No taking this one out all right? Won't take a sec. Give me your arm then. That's it. Now a little scratch. There we are. Didn't feel a thing did you? Right, let's get you hooked up again. You need this. This is your saline. You need it because you're not eating. Right. No taking that out. Are you listening? Right.

*NURSE emerges from the curtains, leaving them drawn. She exits.*

**BRIAN:** It's all go isn't it?

**FRANK:** I beg your pardon.

**BRIAN:** I said it's all go. They're very busy.

**FRANK:** They should be.

**BRIAN:** Do you reckon?

**FRANK:** I've got Parkinson's.

**BRIAN:** Um. Oh. Have you?

**FRANK:** So they said.

**BRIAN:** I see. So you know what's wrong.

**FRANK:** What's wrong? What does he mean, what's wrong?

**BRIAN:** I don't even know. Bit of pain. Bit of blood when I pee. They bring me in here to be looked at but there doesn't seem to be anyone to do any looking. No sign of the lesser spotted Urologist.
An alarm sounds off.

**FRANK:** Now you'll get it. Hear that? Yes. They're coming for you now. Yes, I did call them. You see? Don't look so smart now do you. Eh? You can try to hide your...
What? Don't you bring your drugs in my yard. Do you hear? What?
Oh, bloody hell. Who's glued this?
Oh, you nasty buggers.

*SISTER enters.*

**SISTER:** What are you on about, Frank?

**FRANK:** Someone has glued all this.

**SISTER:** All what?

**FRANK:** All this. This here.

**SISTER:** What? The chair? The chair needs to be glued. It would fall apart otherwise. Now then, Mr Taylor. How are we doing?

**BRIAN:** Well, Do you mind if I could ask you something.

**SISTER:** Fire away.

**BRIAN:** I was just wondering if you knew when I would get seen.

**SISTER:** Seen?

**BRIAN:** By a doctor.

**SISTER:** Haven't you been seen?

**BRIAN:** Not as such. I've been sent for tests. X ray, Ultrasound. But nobody has actually seen me.

**SISTER:** You're under Dr Lyle. He only does three days a week.

**BRIAN:** What? But I've already been here five days, surely he must have been in at some point.

**SISTER:** I wouldn't know, Mr Taylor

**BRIAN:** Is he in today?

**SISTER:** I don't believe he is.

**BRIAN:** Is there no one else I can see?

**SISTER:** Doctors don't like it if we take patients off them. But, I'll see what I can do.

**BRIAN:** Thank you.

**SISTER:** Has she done your vitals?

**BRIAN:** Not yet.

**SISTER:** Sorry, Mr Taylor. We're a bit stretched.

*SISTER exits.*

**FRANK:** Who is she?

**BRIAN:** What's that?

**FRANK:** Her. Who does she think she is?

**BRIAN:** She's the ward sister.

**FRANK:** Is she now?

**BRIAN:** You can tell by the uniform. The darker the blue, the more senior they are. Or maybe the word I should use is superior. More fitting.

**FRANK:** She's your sister?

**BRIAN:** No. She not my sister. She's the senior nurse.

**FRANK:** Oh.

**BRIAN:** She's in charge of the other nurses.

**FRANK:** I thought you said she was your sister.

**BRIAN:** No. She's the ward sister.

**FRANK:** Eh?

*NURSE enters.*

**NURSE:** Right, Mr Taylor. Time to do your vitals.

**BRIAN:** Please, call me Brian.
*During the following NURSE takes BRIAN's "vitals", blood pressure, pulse, respiratory and body temperature.*

**NURSE:** OK.

**BRIAN:** Can I call you Kim?

**NURSE:** Of course.

**BRIAN:** I don't think Sister is very happy with me.

**NURSE:** Really?

**BRIAN:** The thing is, I feel like a bit of a fraud, Kim.

**NURSE:** Why's that?

**BRIAN:** Well, I'm not really ill am I?

**NURSE:** Best to get you checked out though. Blood in your urine isn't it?

**BRIAN:** It was. Seems to have cleared up now.

**NURSE:** What are you doing? Putting the bottles in our room for testing?

**BRIAN:** I have been doing that, yes.

**NURSE:** Well, carry on for now.

**BRIAN:** Sister said Dr Lyle only works three days a week.

**NURSE:** That's right.

**BRIAN:** And he's not in today.

**NURSE:** I think he is, as it happens.

**BRIAN:** Really?

**NURSE:** I think so.

**BRIAN:** Will he come to see me then? I mean, do you think he might?

**NURSE:** I'll let his secretary know you've moved down here. Hopefully, he'll be along later.

*NURSE records BRIAN's results on his chart.*

**BRIAN:** Everything OK?

**NURSE:** Yes, Brian. We must be treating you well.

*NURSE exits with the trolley. BRIAN looks at FRANK who is fidgeting as usual. He puts in his earphones and lies on his bed. PORTER enters with a wheelchair.*

**PORTER:** Taxi for Mr Taylor. Calling Mr Taylor, your time is up. Oh, that can't be right.

**BRIAN:** What?

**PORTER:** Brian Taylor. Ward 12 to Ward 6.

**BRIAN:** I've just come from Ward 6.

**PORTER:** I know you have. I brought you, remember?

**BRIAN:** There must be some mix up.

**PORTER:** Don't worry, I'll sort it. Someone's got their wires crossed, that's all. I'm not taking you back, that's for sure.

**BRIAN:** No, please don't.

**PORTER:** No worries. You'll be all right here. Best ward in the hospital.

**BRIAN:** Is it?

**PORTER:** I mean, it is the same as all the others but it, er has its compensations, if you know what I mean.

*NURSE enters.*

**NURSE:** What are you doing here?

**PORTER:** Lovely to see you too. We were just talking about you.

**NURSE:** Nice things, I hope.

**PORTER:** Naturally.

**NURSE:** So, apart from discussing me with one of my patients, what are you doing here?

**PORTER:** Oh, just one of my wild goose chases.

**NURSE:** Right, well if you've nothing to do you can help me move Mrs Harris? Come on.

**PORTER:** Your wish is my command. (*Nurse exits. To BRIAN.*) What's the difference between a joke and a temperature? A nurse can take a temperature.

*PORTER exits.*

**BRIAN:** Which way are the loos mate?

**FRANK:** What?

**BRIAN:** The toilet. I need the toilet.

**FRANK:** Toilet. Just there (*He points.*)

**BRIAN:** Oh, right. Cheers.

*BRIAN exits taking a urine bottle with him.*

**FRANK:** (*Gently*) They've glued it from the top, right down to the bottom.
Every inch.
Ee dear. What a thing to do.
Ee, fancy that.

## SCENE TWO

*BRIAN is sitting up in his bed listening to his iPod. FRANK is in his chair, asleep. LEN is in his chair, awake but his mind is, as usual, elsewhere. As he sits he gradually slides down in the chair until he almost comes off. At this point he will shout 'Oh bugger' and hold himself in place until somebody props him back up. BRIAN's wife, JUDITH, arrives.*

**JUDITH:** You might have told me you'd moved.

**BRIAN:** (*Removing his earphones.*) I did.

**JUDITH:** You did not.

**BRIAN:** I did. I sent you a text.

**JUDITH:** What good is a text? You know I don't switch my phone on.

**BRIAN:** And I told you that you need to, whilst I'm in here.

**JUDITH:** What for? So I can drop everything and come running whenever you need me?

**BRIAN:** Like you'd do that.

**JUDITH:** The world doesn't revolve around you know, Brian.

**BRIAN:** OK. Whatever.

**JUDITH:** What's wrong with giving me a ring if you need me, anyway? The home phone is always on.

**BRIAN:** We're not supposed to use mobiles. I turned mine on, sent you a text and turned it off again.

**JUDITH:** You could have used the payphone.

**BRIAN:** Look. I told you to keep your mobile turned on. It is a perfectly reasonable request. It's not my fault if you ignore me.

**JUDITH:** Anyone would think you didn't want me to visit.

**BRIAN:** It's up to you. I don't care if you come or not. Why have you come, anyway?

**JUDITH:** Don't worry, it's not a social call.

**BRIAN:** So I gathered. We're past that. I expect that you are quite pleased not to have me in your way.

**JUDITH:** You never were in the way, Brian. In fact you were never there at all. That's our problem.

**BRIAN:** You've just come to have a row, is that it?

**JUDITH:** You started it.

**BRIAN:** No I didn't.

**JUDITH:** Anyway. I don't intend to stay long. I just need to talk to you about Victoria.

**BRIAN:** What's wrong? Is she OK? What's happened?

**JUDITH:** I had another letter from the school.

**BRIAN:** Oh.

**JUDITH:** They want us to go in to see them.

**BRIAN:** Well, I'd love to, of course, but...

**JUDITH:** Oh, don't be pathetic. I haven't come to ask you to hold my hand whilst I go to see the headmaster. I am quite capable of going on my own and we both know what he is going to say, don't we? We know what the problem is, Brian. We've talked about it often enough. She has become disruptive at school because of her disruptive home life. She sees us, at each other's throats all the time, she can't concentrate on her homework, she gets into trouble, she becomes disruptive.

**BRIAN:** Judith, we have agreed that it is best for us to split up. Best for us, and best for Vicky. We've talked about it long and hard and in an uncharacteristic incident of actually being on the same fucking wavelength, for once, we decided on the way forward. I'll find myself somewhere to go and between us, like sensible adults, we'll sort out how and when I see my daughter. Isn't that what we decided? No need to hand over our hard earned cash to solicitors when we are both, usually, capable of being rational without professional help. But my coming in here has made it difficult. We are just going to have to be patient. As soon as I am home I will start looking. Surely you don't expect me to be searching for a flat from my hospital bed?

**JUDITH:** You don't need a flat to move out. You could stay with a friend couldn't you? You do have friends?

**BRIAN:** You're not serious?

**JUDITH:** Even a lowlife like you can have friends.

**BRIAN:** You expect me to find a sofa to sleep on after I leave here?

**JUDITH:** It makes perfect sense. I think it would be best if you didn't come back to the house.

**BRIAN:** I don't believe this. Have you no feelings?

**JUDITH:** She has already got used to you not being around. Not that you were ever there anyway, but you know what I mean. Vicky has now adjusted to the fact that you don't live with us. We should make the most of the situation. It will only upset her if you came back home again.

**BRIAN:** I don't believe I'm hearing this. How can you be so heartless? We still don't know what's wrong with me. I could be seriously ill here. Have you considered that?

**LEN:** Oh, bugger.

**JUDITH:** What's wrong with him?

**BRIAN:** He slides out of the chair. A nurse will come and prop him back up in a minute. Don't you think I've got enough to worry about without you marching in here and telling me that you are throwing me out?

**JUDITH:** Why? You're not really ill are you? Seriously ill, my arse. There's nothing wrong with you.

**BRIAN:** I'm in hospital, Judith.

**JUDITH:** Yes, but you've been OK since you came in. A bit of blood in your piss, that's all it was.

**BRIAN:** We don't know what it was.

**JUDITH:** Bloody typical of you. Only you could spend a week in hospital without anyone seeing you.

*NURSE enters. There is a tense silence between BRIAN and JUDITH until she leaves.*

**NURSE:** Come on then Len. Let's be having you.

*NURSE props LEN up and exits.*

**LEN:** Thank you.

**BRIAN:** I've been having tests.

**JUDITH:** Yeah, yeah. I'm sure you are of academic interest but if there was anything wrong with you you'd have seen a doctor by now. These people know what they are doing, Brian. They know when someone is seriously ill and they deal with it. They don't shunt them round from ward to ward because nobody wants them.

**BRIAN:** Bring her with you tonight.

**JUDITH:** What makes you think I'm coming tonight?

**BRIAN:** I want to speak to her. Send her on the bus if you don't want to come.

**JUDITH:** You think I'd let our daughter come all the way here on her own on the bus? It's a good job one of us is responsible Brian.

**BRIAN:** Then bring her. I want to see her.

**JUDITH:** Oh you do, do you? Well maybe we should have that conversation, about how and when you see your daughter, right now because I'm beginning to think that the less she sees of you the better it will be for her.

**BRIAN:** What?

**JUDITH:** Actually, she hasn't asked about you once since you've been in here.

**BRIAN:** I don't believe you.

**JUDITH:** We are getting on so well without you why change a winning formula?

**BRIAN:** You wouldn't try to stop me from seeing Vicky!

**JUDITH:** I have to think what is best for her.

**BRIAN:** Oh, of course. I can see now that I've been looking at this from the wrong perspective.

**JUDITH:** What?

**BRIAN:** Yes, we have to do what is best for Vicky. In that case why don't you go and sleep on someone's sofa?

**JUDITH:** We agreed that you would leave.

**BRIAN:** I thought it would be easier. That it would disrupt her less. But don't you dare suggest that she is better off with you than she would be with me.

**JUDITH:** So what? Do you intend to parade all your girlfriends in front of her?

**BRIAN:** Here we go.

**JUDITH:** If you think that slut is coming anywhere near my daughter you are very much mistaken.

**BRIAN:** We've been through this a hundred times. Can't you give it a rest?

**JUDITH:** Give it a rest? Were you thinking about giving it a rest whilst you were shagging her?

**BRIAN:** Judith, I've told you...

**JUDITH:** Oh yeah. You were both drunk, it's just one of those things.

**BRIAN:** That isn't what I said.

**JUDITH:** I can't remember what you said. You've told me that many lies they all merge into one. One big lie. That about sums you up, Brian.

**BRIAN:** We. Did. Not. Have. Sex. How many times do I have to tell you?

**JUDITH:** You expect me to believe that?

**BRIAN:** Oh, I don't care what you believe.

**JUDITH:** You just held hands, is that it?

**BRIAN:** She just needed someone to talk to.

**JUDITH:** I'm not interested, Brian.

**BRIAN:** I deceived you. I admitted that. I told you I was some place else when I was with her. That was wrong. I should have told you the truth.

**JUDITH:** Do you even know what the truth is?

**BRIAN:** Well, maybe our marriage was over anyway. Why do you think I had to lie to you, have you thought of that?

**JUDITH:** Are you saying it's my fault?

**BRIAN:** One time I might have been able to say to you, "I've got a friend who needs a chat". You would have understood, you would have trusted me. What happened? What happened to that trust?

**JUDITH:** I can't believe you are still claiming innocence. Admit it, Brian, there's no point in lying about it now.

**BRIAN:** Exactly. That's why you should believe me. I've nothing to gain. We're splitting up. I'm moving out. Why should I lie about it? Nothing happened.

**JUDITH:** Well, we'll see.

**BRIAN:** Yes, we will see. There is no one else. There never has been. There never will be.

**JUDITH:** You're not going to worm your way back in.

**BRIAN:** I don't want to. I'm not trying to. Judith, you are the only woman I ever wanted. I just want you to know the truth.

**JUDITH:** Why?

**BRIAN:** I'm not a bad man, Judith. I think you know that really. I don't know what happened to us. Before all this, I mean. I just...
They look at each other. For a moment there is a hint of tenderness, but it is not to be.

**JUDITH:** I can't come tonight anyway. I've got something on.

**BRIAN:** What?

**JUDITH:** None of your business. I'll bring her tomorrow. Or the next day. If you are still here. Then you have to tell her that you are not coming home.

**BRIAN:** I don't think that is practical.

**JUDITH:** Of course it is practical. Just do it, Brian. Call one of your mates. I'm going. I hate this place.

**BRIAN:** She does ask about me, doesn't she?

**JUDITH:** Yeah, Of course she does.

**BRIAN:** I could text her.

**JUDITH:** Brian, I know you've sent her texts already. She's told me that she has had texts from you. So long as you stick to "Moved wards again, LOL", you can text her as much as you like.

**BRIAN:** She doesn't reply.

**JUDITH:** She never has any credit, and I'm not topping her phone up.

**BRIAN:** But anyway. That's what I meant. I can text her to pass on a message. You don't have to turn your phone on.

**JUDITH:** Oh, how generous. Yeah. Let her know which one of your sad mates you going to move in with.

**BRIAN:** Judith!

**JUDITH:** OK. Sorry! Look, I'm going.

**BRIAN:** Thanks for your visit.

**JUDITH:** Don't be sarcastic, Brian. It doesn't suit you.

*JUDITH exits. BRIAN puts his headphones in. MAUREEN, LEN's wife and ROSIE, his daughter arrive. LEN is slumped down in the chair.*

**MAUREEN:** Oh, Len. How have you managed this? Give me a hand to get him upright, Rosie.

**ROSIE:** Don't you think we should get a nurse, Mum? It's their job.

**MAUREEN:** Oh, what nonsense. Here, grab an arm.

*They lift LEN back to a sitting position.*

**LEN:** Thank you.

**ROSIE:** Hello Dad. (*She kisses him on the cheek. MAUREEN fetches a chair and sits next to her husband. ROSIE sits on the bed.*)

**MAUREEN:** How have you been love? It's nice to see you sitting up. They leave you in that bed too much. You'll get bed sores.

**ROSIE:** You should tell them, Mum.

**MAUREEN:** No. They're very busy. I'm sure they do their best.

**ROSIE:** It is their jobs to look after their patients. Their duty.

**MAUREEN:** You tell them, then.

**ROSIE:** Do you want a drink Dad? (*She pours one.*) Here you are, have a drink.

*ROSIE passes her dad a drink which he shakily takes and sips at. He holds the cup out for her take back which she does.*

**MAUREEN:** So, what have you been up to, Len? What have you been doing?

**LEN:** Sitting here.

**ROSIE:** Nice one, Dad. Sitting there, Mum. That's all he can do.

**MAUREEN:** Well, I don't know. He might have been watching TV.

**ROSIE:** Dad doesn't watch TV.

**MAUREEN:** He might do.

**ROSIE:** Do you want to watch TV, Dad? I can get you one of them cards if you like? Would you like that?

**LEN:** A card?

**ROSIE:** To watch TV.

**LEN:** Eh?

**ROSIE:** They sell them in machines outside. You put them in the TV and you can see the programmes.

**LEN:** I don't want to watch TV.

**ROSIE:** Told you.

**MAUREEN:** Right. Well let's see what you're having for dinner. Pass that sheet, Rosie. (She does.) Oh, you haven't filled it in. You never fill in your dinner sheet. How do they know what to bring you if you don't fill in your sheet?

**LEN:** It all tastes the same anyway.

*ROSIE is amused by this.*

**MAUREEN:** Right. To start. Your choice is tomato soup with a roll or orange juice. Orange juice isn't a starter is it? It's a drink, I'll put soup down. Main course. Shepherd's Pie, chicken, or vegetable curry?

**LEN:** Curry.

**MAUREEN:** I don't think you want curry.

**ROSIE:** Let him have it, if that is what he wants.

**MAUREEN:** It's always given him the runs.

**ROSIE:** I've done curry. He's not had the runs with my curry.

**MAUREEN:** I'll tick shepherd's pie. Now then, chocolate pudding, yoghurt or fruit? No contest there, eh Len? Right. That's done. You're eating better than me.

**ROSIE:** He's not eating at all, Mum. That's why he has to be on a drip.

**MAUREEN:** I'm not surprised if he doesn't tell them what he wants. You have to tick the boxes, Len.

**LEN:** Bugger!

*MAUREEN and ROSIE prop him up again.*

**MAUREEN:** It's not like they're huge portions that they give you. Not enough to feed a mouse. Wait until I get you back home, Len. You'll soon be eating properly when I'm doing the cooking, won't you? I'm doing bacon chops tonight. You'd have eaten that all right.

**ROSIE:** I thought you were coming back with me tonight.

**MAUREEN:** It's all right, Rosie. You can drop me back home.

**ROSIE:** Ah, mum. I thought I was cooking for you.

**MAUREEN:** It's very kind, love, but I can cope on my own.

**ROSIE:** I know you can cope, mum. I isn't a question of whether you can cope. It just makes sense if you come back with me and Steve can drop you home after dinner.

**MAUREEN:** But he doesn't want to be bothered with all that. He's been at work all day. He just wants to come home and have his meal, he doesn't want to go out again to take me home.

**ROSIE:** He doesn't mind. And if he is tired, I can always take you home myself. Tell her, Dad.

**MAUREEN:** Are you sure, dear?

**ROSIE:** Of course. What's brought this on, Mum?

| | |
|---|---|
| **MAUREEN:** | I don't want to be a nuisance. |
| **ROSIE:** | Oh, Mum. You're not a nuisance. We like having you round. Tell her to stop being silly, Dad. |
| **MAUREEN:** | I think he is off to a world of his own. |
| **ROSIE:** | Are you still with us, Dad? |
| **MAUREEN:** | Len. |
| **LEN:** | Eh? |
| **MAUREEN:** | Rosie was talking to you. |
| **LEN:** | Oh. |
| **MAUREEN:** | What are you thinking about? |
| **LEN:** | You. |
| **MAUREEN:** | Me? |
| **ROSIE:** | That's nice. |
| **MAUREEN:** | What are you thinking about me? |
| **LEN:** | I love you. |

*MAUREEN was not expecting this but both she and ROSIE are touched.*

| | |
|---|---|
| **MAUREEN:** | And I love you, Len. |

*MAUREEN takes LEN's hand. ROSIE kisses his forehead. It is very tender.*

| | |
|---|---|
| **ROSIE:** | You old sweetheart. |
| **MAUREEN:** | You always were a romantic at heart, weren't you love? |
| **LEN:** | I should think so. |
| **MAUREEN:** | You should think so? Ha, ha. Oh, Len. You're everything. You are coming home soon? |

| | |
|---|---|
| **ROSIE:** | Don't upset yourself, Mum. |
| **MAUREEN:** | I don't like being on my own. |
| **ROSIE:** | Come on, Mum. You have us. Why don't you stay tonight? |
| **MAUREEN:** | No, dear.<br>The end of visiting time bell goes. |
| **ROSIE:** | Oh, there we are. Time's up, Dad. |
| **LEN:** | Eh? |
| **MAUREEN:** | We'll see you tomorrow love. |
| **ROSIE:** | Unless you want to come tonight, Mum. |
| **MAUREEN:** | I don't think so. |
| **ROSIE:** | That's an idea. Come home with me. Have your dinner then we'll come back for Visiting tonight. Then you can stay the night with us. |
| **MAUREEN:** | It's too much messing about. |
| **ROSIE:** | It's no messing about. I can lend you a nightie if that's what you are worried about. |
| **MAUREEN:** | Thank you for the offer, it's very kind, but your dad likes his routine. It would confuse him if we came tonight. |
| **ROSIE:** | OK. Well, let me know if you change your mind. You will come for dinner, anyway? |
| **MAUREEN:** | Yes, I'll come for dinner. |

*MAUREEN and ROSIE say their goodbyes. SISTER and NURSE enter and put LEN in his bed. SISTER exits. NURSE approaches FRANK.*

| | |
|---|---|
| **NURSE:** | Are you all right in your chair, Frank? Eh? You are? Good job seeing as she's buggered off, I suppose. |
| **FRANK:** | Eh? |
| **NURSE:** | You all right there, Frank? |

**FRANK:** Am I?

**NURSE:** Yes, are you?

**FRANK:** Yes.

**NURSE:** Yes. Good.

*NURSE draws LEN's curtains and exits.*

**FRANK:** You have to wonder sometimes. Who was she?
Her.
That nurse.
The way she talks to me.
I'll tell you who she reminds me of.
That girl. You know.

The one that was, oh. She came back to the school after she'd left to work there.
After she finished as a pupil she came back.
Not teaching. More, helping out, you know.
Pleasant girl.

*JOHN, FRANK's son enters. He has a slightly menacing nature. He takes a chair to FRANK's bedside and sits on it the wrong way round.*

**JOHN:** All right, Dad.

**FRANK:** What?

**JOHN:** Surprised? Not seen me in a while, have you?

**FRANK:** What do you want?

**JOHN:** That's not very nice. Not very welcoming. Aren't you pleased that your only son has come to visit you in hospital?

**FRANK:** Eh?

**JOHN:** It's a bit of a shit hole this, isn't it? You should have gone private. Do you want me to pay for you to go private? I could you know.

**FRANK:** I don't want your money.

**JOHN:** That's not very nice is it? Not a very nice way to speak to your son. You do recognise me don't you? You know who I am?

**FRANK:** I know who you are.

**JOHN:** Good. And don't you forget it. No, you should go private. Be a lot nicer. Wouldn't have to share. I could arrange that for you.

**FRANK:** Why have you come? Where's your mother?

**JOHN:** Mam? Oh, she doesn't know I'm here. No one knows I'm here. Guy on the end is deafening himself with his iPod. Guy in the next bed is probably dead. It's just you and me.

**FRANK:** What do you want?

**JOHN:** Just a chat, Dad. Just a chat.

*The DOCTOR enters and sees LEN's curtains are drawn. He looks at the chart on the end of LEN's bed. He exits speaking to JOHN as he goes.*

**DOCTOR:** Visiting time is over.

**JOHN:** Did you see that? Did you hear him? The way he just spoke to me. Like I'm a piece of shit he has just scraped off the bottom of his shoe. Bunch of Nazis, the lot of them. You don't get that if you go private.

*SISTER enters, tuts and opens LEN's curtains. She speaks to John.*

**SISTER:** I'm sorry, visiting time has just finished. You'll have to come back tonight.

**JOHN:** Oh, I'm sorry, nurse. I've driven up all the way from Southampton and I have to get back tonight. I got delayed on the motorway. Can't I just have ten minutes?

**SISTER:** Well, all right. Ten minutes, but the doctors will be doing their rounds soon so you'll have to leave if they need to speak to Frank.

**JOHN:** Oh thank you. That's very kind.

*SISTER exits.*

**JOHN:** Did you hear that? She called you Frank! No respect.

**FRANK:** I don't want you here.

**JOHN:** Ahh, Dad. I've come all the way from Southampton to see you. Let me stay with you.

**FRANK:** What do you want with me?

**JOHN:** I just want to spend some time with my old Dad. What's wrong with that? Catch up on the gossip. I'm sure you've got plenty of gossip. Me first though; I've got so much to tell you. Business is going really well. The digital switch-over was such a boon to the industry: it's amazing how gullible people can be. Even now I use it as a reason why people need a new aerial. Stupid cunts. Most of them don't think to ask me how come it's worked fine up to now, and if they do I just tell them it's because there has been a grace period. "Haven't you seen the adverts?" I ask them, and they say "Oh, yes." even though I've just made them up. The best one though, Dad? Are you listening? You'll like this. Some old twat rings me up and says he's getting a fuzzy picture and I say I'll come round and when he gives me his address I realise I've already got an appointment to see one of his neighbours. So, I go and see the neighbour first and flog him a new aerial. Two hundred and twenty quid, thank you very much. I sling his old aerial in the van and drive all of fifty yards to this other twat's house and flog him a new aerial as well. Another two hundred and twenty quid – that's four hundred and forty in less than an hour but here's the genius of it all. I flogged the second twat the first twat's old aerial. Can you believe it? There was nowt wrong with it of course, there never is. Aren't you proud of me? Entrepreneurial spirit, they call that. That's how come I can afford to pay for you to go private. That's the difference between you and me, you see. One of the differences. So. What have you been up to then? Dad? Come on, I'm all ears.

**FRANK:** Get out of here.

**JOHN:** What? You don't want to tell me? Come on. I'm interested. How have you been filling your time? Oh. You've not been up to your old tricks have you? Have you? 'Cos you know what? I've heard that you have. That's what I've heard. Even in here. In a hospital. Is that right?

*FRANK is starting to get upset.*

**JOHN:** Got to hand it to you, you're consistent. You know what you like, don't you, Dad? You have your own tastes. Unconventional. Is that what you would call it? You don't let the fact that you're so fucking ancient you should be fucking dead by now get in the way. Never mind the fact that you're in a shit hole NHS hospital 'cos Mam can't cope with you at home. Never mind the fact that you can't even take a piss any more. You sit there with a tube up your dick and your disgusting piss in a plastic bag for all the world to see but (He thinks.) but you are still a man of refinement aren't you, Dad? You still have your preferences. Your little idiosyncrasies. It's a shame, though, that your preference is little girls isn't it, Dad? I mean, in a conventional society it is, shall we say, frowned upon but, probably, it is fine in the sick world that you live in. Nothing wrong with a bit of kiddy fiddling. Isn't that what you think? Haven't changed have you? A paedo in charge of a school! It's no surprise that you never wanted to retire. What do you do now? Do you sneak off to the kiddies ward in the middle of the night? Dragging your bag of piss with you. Is that how you get your kicks?

*With a tremendous effort FRANK launches himself at John and they both end up on the floor. BRIAN hears the commotion and jumps up from his bed.*

**BRIAN:** Jesus!

*BRIAN goes to try to help FRANK as SISTER and NURSE also arrive. They get FRANK back in his chair where he sits sobbing. JOHN goes for FRANK.*

**JOHN:** What the fuck do you think you're doing? I'll fucking kill you, you bastard. You think you have the right to attack me? After what you did?

*BRIAN tries to restrain JOHN as PORTER arrives.*

**PORTER:** Come on.

**NURSE:** Get him out of here.

**PORTER:** Come on.

**FRANK:** Miserere nobis, miserere nobis. (*Have mercy on us.*)

**JOHN:** He's a fucking nut case. What are you fucking talking about, you cunt?

**PORTER:** You'll have to come with me or I'll call security.

**JOHN:** It's him you want to lock up. He should have been put away years ago. Do you know what he did?

**NURSE:** I'll call security.

**JOHN:** Don't bother, I'm going. Hear that, Dad? They're going to call security for me!

*JOHN frees himself from the clutches of BRIAN and PORTER and makes to exit.*

**JOHN:** Just check his background. His fondness for little girls. See what sort of a man he is. Fucking perv. You won't feel so sorry for him then.

*JOHN exits. SISTER follows. PORTER helps FRANK recover.*

**SISTER:** I'll see you out.

**FRANK:** Miserere nobis.

**NURSE:** I'm so sorry Brian. We've never had anything like this happen before.

**BRIAN:** Not your fault. What it was all about?

**NURSE:** Thanks for your help. You shouldn't have got involved though.

**BRIAN:** Well I couldn't just sit there. I wish I hadn't had my earphones in. I might have been able to stop it sooner.

| | |
|---|---|
| **NURSE:** | You didn't hear any of it then? |
| **BRIAN:** | Nothing before they both ended up on the floor. Did you? |
| **NURSE:** | (Quickly) No. |
| **BRIAN:** | From what I saw it looked like Frank launched himself at that guy. |
| **NURSE:** | He should never have been allowed in here. |
| **BRIAN:** | But, about what that guy was saying... |
| **NURSE:** | At least we got it under control quickly. |
| **PORTER:** | Lucky I was passing. |
| **FRANK:** | Our Father. Who art in Heaven. Hallowed be thy name. |
| **NURSE:** | Yes. Why were you passing? |
| **PORTER:** | I've got a patient to move. (He takes a note from his pocket and reads it. To Brian.) Oh bollocks. Pardon my French. It's you again isn't it! |

## SCENE THREE

*Curtains are drawn around LEN's bed. BRIAN is lying on his bed listening to his iPod. FRANK is in his chair.*

**FRANK:** Bloody buggers.
Coming in my yard. I know who you are, you know.
I'll have the law onto you.
Don't think I won't.
I'm watching you. Watching all the time.
I see it all. See what you do.

*BRIAN takes off iPod gets up and exits, speaking to FRANK on the way.*

**BRIAN:** You all right mate?

**FRANK:** Eh? What does he mean?
You think you can pull one over me?
An old man?

| | |
|---|---|
| **FRANK:** | Ee dear.<br>Bloody buggers. I can see you.<br>I didn't mean it, you know. No harm was meant.<br>I didn't do any harm. I saw her.<br>You understand that don't you? You know what I mean?<br>Ah, they've bloody glued all this. What? Why? What do they want to glue this for?<br>She's was all right. No harm done.<br>I saw her, you see. I could have taken it further. Perhaps I should have done.<br>I don't know.<br>I don't know.<br>But when it's one of your own. You think you can work it out.<br>No need for it now. It's all Facebooks.<br>Twitter and Facebooks. |

*BRIAN enters.*

| | |
|---|---|
| **BRIAN:** | Facebook, Frank? |
| **FRANK:** | Eh? |
| **BRIAN:** | You on Facebook are you? Into all that are you? Social media. |
| **FRANK:** | I know about Facebook. |
| **BRIAN:** | You're full of surprises. |
| **FRANK:** | Eh? |
| **BRIAN:** | You're a bit of an enigma. |
| **FRANK:** | Me? |
| **BRIAN:** | What was that about yesterday? |
| **FRANK:** | Yesterday? |
| **BRIAN:** | Your visitor. |
| **FRANK:** | He's a fool. |
| **BRIAN:** | He's a maniac, I know that. Want to talk about it? |

**FRANK:** He shouldn't be allowed in here.

**BRIAN:** I don't think he will be allowed in again.

*BRIAN drags a visitor's chair over and sits with FRANK.*

**BRIAN:** So. Frank. About what he was saying?

**FRANK:** They should have thrown away the key.

**BRIAN:** He's been inside?

**FRANK:** Not fit to be in society.

**BRIAN:** He's been in prison?

**FRANK:** He should have been.

**BRIAN:** What he was saying? About? Girls? You know, it was difficult to make out what he meant but... Well. I mean, he said... He suggested that there was a problem. With girls.

**FRANK:** I told him. You should be locked up. What he did.

**BRIAN:** Him?

**FRANK:** What?

**BRIAN:** He should be locked up? It was because... It's him?

**FRANK:** Him?

**BRIAN:** In prison. He should have gone to prison?

**FRANK:** Oh, yes.

**BRIAN:** Because of the, er, business with girls.

**FRANK:** Girls?

**BRIAN:** Your son.

**FRANK:** He's not my son.

**BRIAN:** No, well. I can understand you feeling like that.

**FRANK:** He's not my son.

**BRIAN:** You mean he really isn't your son? Who is he then?

**FRANK:** A father.

**BRIAN:** A father. Who's father? A father of one of the girls? Who should have gone to prison?

**FRANK:** I'm a father myself. Only had the one.
It's a boy! I always wanted a girl you know. But she wouldn't have any more.
Not going through that again.
It was difficult, you know.
Not the birth.
Well, yes. The birth, but what came after as well.
No more, she said.
No more.

**BRIAN:** My wife had a difficult time with Victoria. Came out backwards, you know. Different in your day, of course.

**FRANK:** She wanted to kill him. He's not mine she said. Not mine.

**BRIAN:** Oh right. Post Natal Depression.

**FRANK:** Eh?

**BRIAN:** After the birth. Your wife was depressed.

**FRANK:** She wasn't depressed.

**BRIAN:** No?

**FRANK:** After she found out what he did. She wanted to kill him.

**BRIAN:** Your son?

**FRANK:** He did that to you? I'll kill him.
He was always bad.
He thinks I don't know what he gets up to.

**BRIAN:** What did he get up to?

**FRANK:** Eh?

**BRIAN:** Your son. What did he get up to?

**FRANK:** My son? Do you know my son?

**BRIAN:** He was here yesterday. Him, yesterday. That was your son?

**FRANK:** Eh?

*NURSE enters.*

**BRIAN:** The guy here yesterday.

**FRANK:** What does he mean?

**NURSE:** He doesn't mean anything, Frank. He's just looking out for you.

**FRANK:** Looking out for me?

**NURSE:** That's it.

**FRANK:** I don't need a look out.

**BRIAN:** See you later, Frank.

*BRIAN returns to his bed. NURSE tidies FRANK's bedding, opens the curtains around LEN's bed, which is unoccupied, and makes it up. She is cool with BRIAN – unhappy that he has been probing.*

**BRIAN:** Is he doing OK? Len?

**NURSE:** I've not heard.

**BRIAN:** Will they keep him in intensive care now?

**NURSE:** Depends on the beds. Like everything else. If they are short of beds he'll come back here.

**BRIAN:** He gave us a bit of a fright last night. I thought we'd had enough drama for one day.

*NURSE doesn't respond.*

**BRIAN:** It was impressive though. How professional everyone became. Saved his life.

**NURSE:** That's what we are here for.

**BRIAN:** Bet you're glad it wasn't on your shift.

**NURSE:** We have to take what comes. Save a life, you're a hero: save a hundred lives, you're a nurse.

*NURSE passes close to BRIAN as she is about to leave.*

**BRIAN:** I assume that was his son last night.

**NURSE:** I believe so, yes.

**BRIAN:** What he was saying? Was it? I mean, is there any...

**NURSE:** I can't really talk about it.

**BRIAN:** I know but... That stuff he was saying. Was there anything in it? I mean, you never know do you? The thing is, I'm expecting a visit from my daughter and...

**NURSE:** She'll be perfectly safe.

**BRIAN:** That's not what I mean. I know. I know she'll be safe. But I don't want here her if he...

**NURSE:** Don't worry.

**BRIAN:** It's just that. The guy last night. I mean. Frank said something about a father. If the guy who came last night was the father of... I mean, if he wasn't Frank's son, but the father of someone who...

**NURSE:** Look. Don't worry about Frank. And his son won't be coming back.

**BRIAN:** You're sure it was his son?

**NURSE:** Yes.

**BRIAN:** And, what? Frank's son was accusing his dad of child abuse when it is actually himself?

**NURSE:** I really don't know very much about it. To put your mind at rest, there is nothing on Frank's records to say that he is a risk. OK? I shouldn't be telling you that, but I can see that you're concerned and I don't want you probing my patient.

**BRIAN:** No. of course. Sorry.

**NURSE:** It's OK.

*NURSE exits. BRIAN puts his iPod on. FRANK fidgets. A moment passes. JUDITH and VICTORIA enter.*

**JUDITH:** Take it easy why don't you?

**VICTORIA:** Dad!

*BRIAN removes his earphones delighted to see his daughter.*

**BRIAN:** Hello sweetheart.

**VICTORIA:** I've missed you, Dad. When are you coming home?

**BRIAN:** I've missed you too, sweetheart. Would you believe I haven't even seen a doctor yet? I might as well be at home.

**VICTORIA:** You can come home with us now. Can't he, mum?

**BRIAN:** I really ought to wait. It will be today, hopefully. So what have you been up to?

**VICTORIA:** The usual, you know.

**BRIAN:** Oh yeah. I thought the jet ski was broken. And you've not been flying your helicopter before you've finished your homework, I hope.

**VICTORIA:** Only once or twice. But mostly...

**BRIAN:** Yeah?

**VICTORIA:** Mostly I've been playing Angry Birds*.
*(or current craze)

**JUDITH:** Did you want anything from the shop?

**BRIAN:** Eh?

**JUDITH:** I'm going to the shop. Do you want anything?

**VICTORIA:** I'll go, mum.

**JUDITH:** No, you stay, Vickie. Your father has something to tell you. Well?

**BRIAN:** Judith, I don't think...

**JUDITH:** Do you want anything?

**BRIAN:** No.

**JUDITH:** Right. Well I'll be ten minutes. You know what you need to do.

*JUDITH exits.*

**VICTORIA:** What's up with her?

**BRIAN:** She's just a bit tense, that's all.

**VICTORIA:** She's a cow.

**BRIAN:** Now, Vic. You mustn't talk like that about your mother.

**VICTORIA:** You should hear what she says about you.

**BRIAN:** Well. Things aren't too good between us at the moment.

**VICTORIA:** You're telling me.

**BRIAN:** Vic, you are almost an adult now, so there is no point in treating you like a child.

**VICTORIA:** Yeah...?

**BRIAN:** So. You will have noticed that the relationship between your mother and I has deteriorated a lot recently and, for some time, we have found living together quite difficult.

**VICTORIA:** What are you saying, Dad?

**BRIAN:** The thing is. Look, there is no easy way of putting this.

**VICTORIA:** No easy way of putting what?

**BRIAN:** The thing is...

**VICTORIA:** Hang on.

**BRIAN:** Your mum and me...

**VICTORIA:** Oh no!

**BRIAN:** Vic.

**VICTORIA:** Don't say it. Don't say it!

**BRIAN:** I'm sorry, Vic.

**VICTORIA:** You're getting a divorce!

**BRIAN:** I don't know what to say. Sorry.

**VICTORIA:** Sorry!

**BRIAN:** Vic...

**VICTORIA:** You're sorry?

**BRIAN:** Please...

**VICTORIA:** Fuck my life up, why don't you?

**BRIAN:** Vic.

**VICTORIA:** Great. My parents are getting a divorce. Bollocks to my exams. So, you hate each other? So what? Most married couples hate each other, don't they?

**BRIAN:** Vic, calm down. I know this is difficult. And this isn't the best way to have to tell you.

**VICTORIA:** Yeah. Why are you telling me now, Dad? What's the point? Why not wait till you get home? Wait until the summer? Choose your moment. Jesus!

**BRIAN:** Well, we thought that. I might...

**VICTORIA:** What? What did you think, Dad?

**BRIAN:** It's just that I don't know how long I'm going to be in here. Not long hopefully, but when I do leave....

**VICTORIA:** Yeah?

**BRIAN:** I thought I might go to Jim's.

**VICTORIA:** Jim?

**BRIAN:** You know. Jim from the quiz team.

**VICTORIA:** Yeah. I know who Jim is. I'm not thick. What's going on, Dad?

**BRIAN:** If I come home, I'm bound to be off work for a bit. Under your mum's feet. So...

**VICTORIA:** So you're not coming home.

**BRIAN:** No.

**VICTORIA:** Fucking great. Fucking marvellous.

**BRIAN:** I'm really sorry, Victoria.

**VICTORIA:** Has she put you up to this? She has, hasn't she? It's her idea.

**BRIAN:** We just thought it best...

**VICTORIA:** Don't give me that. Wait a minute. She's told you to tell me you're not coming home. That's why she gone to the shop. The coward can't even stand to be here whilst you do her dirty business. Why don't you stand up to her, Dad?

**BRIAN:** It's. Complicated.

**VICTORIA:** Complicated? What's complicated?

**BRIAN:** Your mum is very angry with me at the moment.

**VICTORIA:** Yeah? Well, so am I. Have either of you considered me in this? I thought we were a family. You say that I'm almost an adult, so treat me like one. Can't we sit down and talk about this and decide what is best? Isn't that what families do? Or don't you care? Are you so frightened of her, you just do what she tells you?

**BRIAN:** I'm sorry.

**VICTORIA:** So you're not coming home. I can't understand why you need to do this now. How long have you been married?

**BRIAN:** Yes, but we are facing a kind of crisis and…

**VICTORIA:** Hang on. Why did you say she's angry with you "at the moment"? Why?

**BRIAN:** It's just a - misunderstanding, that's all.

**VICTORIA:** A misunderstanding. What the fuck does that mean?

**BRIAN:** It means a misunderstanding. You don't need to know.

**VICTORIA:** Oh thanks. Don't mind me. I'm just your daughter. My parents are getting a divorce because of a little misunderstanding. (As though she is speaking to someone else.) No, I don't know what it is – they didn't tell me, so it can't have been anything important. I expect it is just something like, um, my father forgot to pick up some milk on his way home so there was none for the coffee, or my mother thought that my father had put out the wheelie bin and he thought she had, so it didn't get collected. Such a nuisance. I know it sounds trivial, but it really can't have been more than that, otherwise I'm sure they would have told me.

**BRIAN:** I don't mean that you don't need to know.

**VICTORIA:** That's what you just said!

**BRIAN:** I mean that it is something trivial. It's unimportant.

**VICTORIA:** Dad! It can't be unimportant if it is the reason you are splitting up!

**BRIAN:** I went for a drink with a mate.

**VICTORIA:** So?

**BRIAN:** I didn't tell you mum.

**VICTORIA:** And? What? She wondered where you were?

**BRIAN:** She found out that I had been for a drink and, because I hadn't told her, she jumped to conclusions.

**VICTORIA:** Hang on. I'm missing something here? Oh! I see. This "mate"...

**BRIAN:** A woman.

**VICTORIA:** Christ, Dad!

**BRIAN:** We've become quite close, but she is just a mate, believe me.

**VICTORIA:** Yeah. Of course I believe you. What is suspicious about that?

**BRIAN:** It's the truth.

**VICTORIA:** How many times did you "go for a drink"?

**BRIAN:** Just the once.

**VICTORIA:** And how many times did you shag her?

**BRIAN:** Believe me, Vic. I wouldn't lie to you.

**VICTORIA:** Does mum believe you?

**BRIAN:** What do you think?

**VICTORIA:** Are you telling me the truth, Dad?

| | |
|---|---|
| **BRIAN:** | I am, Vic. Honestly. My friend just needed someone to talk to. It was nothing. |
| **VICTORIA:** | So, you're getting a divorce over nothing? Why you? |
| **BRIAN:** | What? |
| **VICTORIA:** | Why did your friend choose you to talk to? Doesn't she have any other friends? |
| **BRIAN:** | I think she just thought I'd be a good listener. |
| **VICTORIA:** | It's a bit odd though isn't it? I mean, if I needed to talk to someone about something I would probably either talk to you about it or to one of my girlfriends. |
| **BRIAN:** | Everyone's different. |
| **VICTORIA:** | Why did she choose you, Dad? |
| **BRIAN:** | Because… Because it concerned me. |
| **VICTORIA:** | Ah! So, not just because you are a good listener then? |
| **BRIAN:** | No. She wanted to clear the air, that's all. |
| **VICTORIA:** | What does that mean? |
| **BRIAN:** | I said that we'd become quite close. It was just a case of working out where we stood. |
| **VICTORIA:** | I see. |
| **BRIAN:** | I shouldn't be burdening you with this, Vic. This isn't right. |
| **VICTORIA:** | Have you told Mum this? |
| **BRIAN:** | I've tried. |
| **VICTORIA:** | She wouldn't listen to you? |
| **BRIAN:** | It isn't her fault. Anyone would react the same way. |
| **VICTORIA:** | I'm not. Tell me, Dad. I'm listening. |

**BRIAN:** It won't do any good.

**VICTORIA:** I don't care. If you and Mum are splitting up I want to know why.

**BRIAN:** I asked her to go for a drink with me.

**VICTORIA:** And?

**BRIAN:** She did.

**VICTORIA:** Don't be funny, Dad. Why did you ask her to go for a drink with you?

**BRIAN:** Like I said. To work out where we stood. She had become very fond of me.

**VICTORIA:** So you were trying to decide whether to leave us and move in with her. Is that it?

**BRIAN:** No. I would never… I had no interest. But, it was obvious that she was… What I mean is that she misread the situation. I was just being friendly towards her and she thought…

**VICTORIA:** When you say "Work out where we stood", you really mean tell her where she stood.

**BRIAN:** No. I suppose so, yes.

**VICTORIA:** So why don't you say that?

**BRIAN:** I don't know, it's…

**VICTORIA:** You're too nice, that's your trouble. You said it like that to spare your friend's feelings and she's not even here. So what did you tell her?

**BRIAN:** Just that I was sorry if she'd got the wrong impression but… but there was nothing doing.

**VICTORIA:** And that's everything?

**BRIAN:** Yes.

**VICTORIA:** No it isn't.

**BRIAN:** What?

**VICTORIA:** How did she get the wrong impression?

**BRIAN:** Oh.

**VICTORIA:** Come on, Dad.

**BRIAN:** OK. I… We… Just once we, we were celebrating something and, and there was a moment.

**VICTORIA:** A moment?

**BRIAN:** Yes. Everyone was hugging each other and…

**VICTORIA:** You had a snog.

**BRIAN:** Um…

**VICTORIA:** You had a snog, she thought she was in and you had to put her right. Is that it?

**BRIAN:** I suppose. In a nutshell.

**VICTORIA:** How did Mum find out?

**BRIAN:** Someone saw us. Some kind soul decided she had to ask your mum who the woman was that I was having a drink with.

**VICTORIA:** Which pub did you go in?

**BRIAN:** The Traveller's Rest.

**VICTORIA:** For fuck's sake, Dad. Couldn't you go anywhere else? You're shit at deception.

**BRIAN:** It was never my intention to deceive anyone.

**VICTORIA:** And for this you are getting a divorce.

**BRIAN:** Not just that.

**VICTORIA:** What! How many others were there?

**BRIAN:** No one. I mean, I guess it's been coming for a while. Your mum and me.

**VICTORIA:** What do you mean?

**BRIAN:** You know things haven't been great, Vic.

**VICTORIA:** And you've given her an excuse to kick you out.

**BRIAN:** The way your mother sees it...

**VICTORIA:** But you're innocent?

**BRIAN:** Well. Yes.

**VICTORIA:** So, stand up to her, Dad. Tell her what you told me. She'll forgive you one snog, surely.

**BRIAN:** I've tried, Vic. I really don't want to leave you. You know that.

**VICTORIA:** Try harder.

**BRIAN:** It's too late.

**VICTORIA:** Why doesn't she go? Why do you have to leave?

**BRIAN:** That isn't how it works.

**VICTORIA:** I want to live with you, not her. If I have to chose.

**BRIAN:** It isn't practical...

**VICTORIA:** Fuck practical! I'm almost adult, you said.

**BRIAN:** Vic. Try to keep calm. And your language, please. You shouldn't speak to me like that.

**VICTORIA:** You're bothered about my language all of a sudden! Fuck, fuck fuck fuck fuck. Cunt.

**BRIAN:** Please.

**VICTORIA:** What? Are people looking at us?

**BRIAN:** I don't care if people are looking at us. I'm sorry, Vic. This isn't the place.

**VICTORIA:** Exactly my point, but you're telling me all this now because she told you to. Well, I'm not going home with her.

**BRIAN:** Vic.

**VICTORIA:** I'm staying here, with you. I'll sleep in the chair. And when you go to Jim's, I'll go with you. We can both sleep on the sofa.

**BRIAN:** You can't, Vic. Things will sort themselves out. She's a good mum. And she loves you, you know she does. You do don't you? She thinks the world of you. It would break her heart if you moved out and I'll see you all the time. That's a promise.

*VICTORIA's resolve breaks and she begins to cry. She is a child again.*

**VICTORIA:** Dad.

**BRIAN:** Come here.

*They hug. FRANK half sings, half recites.*

**FRANK:** Glory be to God on high and on earth peace good will towards men we praise thee.
You must think I'm soft.
Yes you! I'm talking to you.
Don't look at your mother.
What?
That was a nasty trick you pulled. A nasty trick.

**FRANK:** Thou takest away the sins of the world, receive our prayer.
Receive our prayer.

## SCENE FOUR

*The curtains around LEN's bed are closed. FRANK is asleep. BRIAN is sitting on his bed typing into a laptop. NURSE enters with MAUREEN and ROSIE.*

**NURSE:** Take as much time as you want. I'll be at my station if you need me.

*NURSE exits. Out of respect BRIAN stops typing. MAUREEN and ROSIE pull open LEN's curtain enough for them to be seen.*

**ROSIE:** Doesn't he look peaceful?

**MAUREEN:** Why do you say that? What a stupid thing to say. People always say stupid things.

**ROSIE:** Sorry, Mum.

**MAUREEN:** Course he looks peaceful. He's hardly likely to be doing the Hokey Cokey is he?

**ROSIE:** No.

**MAUREEN:** Oh, Len.

**ROSIE:** I'll leave you alone for a bit.

**MAUREEN:** I'm sorry, Rosie. I shouldn't have snapped.

**ROSIE:** It's OK, Mum. I'll leave you with Dad.

**MAUREEN:** No, don't go. Stay for a bit.

*ROSIE fetches a chair and they sit.*

**ROSIE:** Are you alright, Mum?

**MAUREEN:** Yes. Well, I will be. Look at him. Do you remember, he was always one for joining clubs? The Caravan Club, The Camping and Caravan Club, English Heritage, The National Trust. I wouldn't mind but he kept up the membership for years after we sold the caravan. And he never did like visiting stately homes. He just liked looking at the catalogues. Well now I've joined a club.

|  |  |
|---|---|
|  | Not a very exclusive one. The Widows' Club. Do you know how many men live to Len's age? Not many. I'm lucky I suppose. If he'd had a manual job he would have gone years ago with asbestos poisoning or some other horrible industrial disease. |
| **ROSIE:** | Dad loved his job didn't he? |
| **MAUREEN:** | I wouldn't go that far. He was proud when he got his qualification though. "There will always be work for an accountant", he told me. That was before computers, of course, but he didn't let that get in the way. I think he was using a computer to do his job whilst the rest of the world was still on an abacus. (*She smiles.*) He used to tell me off for saying that. "Accountants don't count numbers, it's bookkeepers that do that. Accountants present information. I'll never lose my job to a computer, but a bookkeeper might." He always insisted on making the distinction. But he was happy enough when it came to retirement. Bought the caravan with his lump sum and never looked back. |
| **ROSIE:** | Dan and Kate loved the caravan. |
| **MAUREEN:** | I'd never seen him so happy. He would make out that was to give you and Steve a break but we both knew the truth. Having the children with us made us both feel young again. I think that was the happiest time of our lives. Good while it lasted. |

*Silence. MAUREEN is brooding. ROSIE is uncomfortable.*

| | |
|---|---|
| **MAUREEN:** | You can leave me. I can see that you are itching to go. |

*ROSIE is about to argue but realises there is no point.*

| | |
|---|---|
| **ROSIE:** | Don't be long, Mum. |
| **MAUREEN:** | Why? Have you got an appointment? Somewhere you need to be? I can get the bus home. |
| **ROSIE:** | You know that's not what I meant. It's just that I don't think it's a good idea to sit here for too long. |

**MAUREEN:** What else have I got to do? Oh, you mean I have to get on with my life. Move on?

**ROSIE:** No. I don't know why I said it. It was a silly thing to say. Sorry. Take as long as you like.

**MAUREEN:** Perhaps you should go, Rosie. I can get the bus. Really, I can. I've got change.

**ROSIE:** Not today, Mum.

**MAUREEN:** Isn't that what you said before? It's time to move on.

**ROSIE:** That was a long time ago, Mum.

**MAUREEN:** I know it was a long time ago. It broke your Dad's heart.

**ROSIE:** Mum…

**MAUREEN:** How can you sit there and say Kate loved the caravan when you banned her from coming with us.

**ROSIE:** I meant she loved it when she was little.

**MAUREEN:** She never grew out of it. She always loved coming with us.

**ROSIE:** Because you were too soft on her. Teenage girls need discipline.

**MAUREEN:** Of course, your Dad and me knew nothing about bringing up children.

**ROSIE:** We've been over this again and again, Mum. I thought we'd…

**MAUREEN:** Moved on?

**ROSIE:** I'm really sorry it upset you so much. We didn't stop Kate from visiting you.

**MAUREEN:** That's why Len sold the caravan. Dan had lost interest and Kate wasn't allowed.

**ROSIE:** If you had just waited a bit. Waited until Kate got over her rebellious stage.

**MAUREEN:** I wasn't enough for him.

**ROSIE:** That's not true.

**MAUREEN:** It's how it felt at the time. I thought I'd never forgive him. But I did. You don't stay married to someone for nearly sixty years without a bit of forgiveness.

**ROSIE:** I'll try to remember that!

**MAUREEN:** Of course you married young as well didn't you? Not as young as me though. My mother, your grandmother, said it would never last. That I only wanted to get married because I was going through my "rebellious stage".

**ROSIE:** I'll go along to the day room. Stay as long as you like, Mum. Bye, Dad. I'm going to miss you.

*ROSIE kisses her father then partially closes the curtain leaving it open enough for MAUREEN to be seen. MAUREEN stands by the bed. ROSIE exits.*

**MAUREEN:** Well, Len, this is it then. Didn't keep your promise did you? Don't die before me, I said. We knew that wasn't going to happen didn't we? Like I said to Rosie, it's always the wives that are left behind. And no, it isn't because men do all the bloody work no matter how many times you said it. (*Pause*) I'm sorry I was so hard on Rosie. I don't even know why I had to drag up all that business about Kate again. I remember how angry you were when she said Kate couldn't come with us but it wasn't what you thought was it? We were too soft on her if we are honest. And we didn't even tell Rosie about most of the things she got up to. (*Pause*) I was angry with you for selling the caravan. And I know you regretted it. It isn't often you do something impetuous but when you do, my God! Why didn't we get another one, Len? Why be a member of the club and not own a caravan? Still, it would have to go eventually wouldn't it? And we did all right. We didn't need anyone else did we? And now it's just me. What am I going to do, Len? What am I going to do?

*MAUREEN starts to sob. SISTER goes to her.*

**SISTER:** (*Gently*) Is there anything I can get you?

**MAUREEN:** No. I just. I don't...

**SISTER:** Is your daughter here? Shall I fetch her?

**MAUREEN:** No. She's here but I don't want her to see me.

**SISTER:** Why ever not?

**MAUREEN:** I have to be strong. For her sake.

**SISTER:** You just think about yourself.

**MAUREEN:** I don't know what I'm going to do. Sixty years we were married. Sixty! Nearly. Never apart. Never a night apart until he came in here. I still ask him if he wants a cup of tea now. I'm in the kitchen and I shout to him and when I come through to see why he hasn't answered I remember. Four months he has been in here. The longest four months of my life. But now it's going to last forever.

**SISTER:** I know it seems impossible at the moment, but you will find a way to go on. You will always have your memories.

**MAUREEN:** What use are memories?

**SISTER:** It sounds like you had a very happy marriage.

**MAUREEN:** There was never anyone else. Except Rosie, of course. And her Steve and their children. Except they are grown up of course. Len would have been a great granddad in a few more months...

**SISTER:** Sounds lovely.

**MAUREEN:** I'm lucky. Is that what you're saying? I suppose you are right, I know I was lucky. You see so many divorces. Lying, cheating. But not Len. Or Steve. Must be something in the genes, he always said. Something I passed onto to Rosie - the ability to pick a good man.

**SISTER:** Are you stopping with Rosie at the moment?

**MAUREEN:** They don't want me under their feet.

**SISTER:** I'm sure they wouldn't mind.

**MAUREEN:** Why wouldn't they mind? They have their own lives.

**SISTER:** Perhaps they would like to have you staying with them.

**MAUREEN:** They say that.

**SISTER:** Well then?

**MAUREEN:** Rosie is trying to do the right thing. To do her duty. No, that's not fair. She wants to repay me, I suppose. We're a traditional family. You look after your children and then, when you are old, they look after you. That's the way she's been brought up. But I don't want looking after. Len's been part of my life for sixty years but, now that he's gone, it doesn't mean that I need to replace him with Rosie. I don't know how I'm going to do it but I'm going to do it on my own

**SISTER:** That's why you wouldn't stay with her whilst Len's been in here?

**MAUREEN:** How do you know that? Oh, I see. She's had a word has she?

**SISTER:** She's just worried about you.

**MAUREEN:** So she's asked you to come and make me see sense.

**SISTER:** Nothing like that. She didn't ask me to speak to you.

**MAUREEN:** So why did you?

**SISTER:** We all grew quite fond of Len. He always had a bit of a twinkle in his eye, didn't he? A bit of a mischievous streak. He could have the nurses in stitches. He thought the world of you, he told me himself. When I first started in nursing I used to get upset when we lost a patient. I nearly gave up. It's part of the job and I couldn't cope with it. But then I found a way to cope. I distanced

|  |  |
|---|---|
|  | myself. People think I'm cold. Efficient. I've been called heartless by both staff and patients. But I'm good at my job and that's what counts. Len saw through it all. He knew I was putting up a front. Even though I wouldn't admit it he just said, "Don't worry. It will be our secret". And he told me all about you and how he'd promised that he wouldn't die first, knowing that it was a promise he couldn't keep. He told me that you were preparing yourself for the fact that he wouldn't be going home by trying to get used to life on your own, even though Rosie begged you to go and stay with her. He never doubted strength, you would adapt to life without him. The one thing that worried him was Rosie. He said that he was always the peacemaker. |
| MAUREEN: | Did he, now? Well, some of the time, I suppose. |
| SISTER: | He wanted me to tell you to go gentle on her. I shouldn't have agreed, really, but he can be very persuasive. |
| MAUREEN: | He's a crafty one. All right, Len. I'll stay with her for a couple of days. While we sort out the funeral. Then I'll go home. If she's up to it. |
| SISTER: | Do you need anything? |
| MAUREEN: | No. I'll just say goodbye. |

*Sister exits.*

| | |
|---|---|
| MAUREEN: | Where would I be without you eh, Len? Don't worry. I'll be all right. Keep a place for me, won't you? Goodnight Len. |

## SCENE FIVE

*LEN's bed is made and the curtains pushed back. FRANK is alone in the ward.*

| | |
|---|---|
| FRANK: | What have they done here? It's all glued. What do you want to do that for? Buggers.<br>I can see you. Don't look at your mother. She can't help you. Coming in my yard. What? What are you doing to her? That's a nasty trick. (Sings) Fairest Lord Jesus, Ruler of all nature, O Thou of God and man the Son. Let her go. What's wrong with her?<br>Doing drugs in my yard. Giving her drugs. |

**FRANK:** Get her out of here. And you. Go. Don't come back. Yes, you. I know who you are. You're no son of mine. I couldn't.
I know, I know. I should have done. Should have reported it. Put a stop to it. Then he wouldn't.
I'm so sorry. So sorry.
Those kiddies. How could you?
I should have put an end to it. I should have called them. Taking advantage.
How could you? Such a nasty trick. A nasty trick you pulled.
(*Sings*) Fairest Lord Jesus, Ruler of all nature, O Thou of God and man the Son, Thee will I cherish, Thee will I honour, Thou, my soul's glory, joy and crown.
What? What have they done to this? Taking advantage. Clear off. Using my yard.
(*Sings*) Breathe on me, breath of God, Fill me with life anew, that I may love what thou dost love, and do what thou wouldst do.
I'm sorry.
I'm so sorry.

## SCENE SIX

FRANK *fidgets in his chair.* BRIAN *is dressed.* NURSE *enters.*

**NURSE:** You're leaving us then?

**BRIAN:** Yes. Just waiting for my prescription to be ready.

**NURSE:** Oh, right. You've ordered an evening meal then? Joke. It shouldn't be too long. Home cooking for you tonight, eh?

**BRIAN:** I'm not so sure about that.

**NURSE:** Or a takeaway?

**BRIAN:** I don't even know where I'm going. I tried to get hold of my mate but I think he must be away.

**NURSE:** You're not going home?

**BRIAN:** I kind of made an agreement with my wife. As we are splitting up anyway, we might as well make a clean breast of it.

**NURSE:** But we can't discharge you if you haven't got anywhere to go.

**BRIAN:** I'll be all right.

**NURSE:** No, I mean, really. It's against the rules.

**BRIAN:** Oh. I see.

**NURSE:** Maybe if you explained to her that there is nowhere for you to go... Sorry. None of my business.

**BRIAN:** I'm not sure.

**NURSE:** You can stay in you know. We kind of assume that people will want to go home if the doctor says they can but, as we haven't actually found the cause of your problems, you could stay a few more nights. I mean, do you want me to have a word?

**BRIAN:** What about the bed situation?

**NURSE:** That's OK. There isn't actually a shortage of beds in this hospital, just a shortage of staff. That's why you kept getting shunted from ward to another. Just to keep the patient numbers down. But you don't use up much resource. You're no trouble. Well, not much anyway.

**BRIAN:** It might be an idea of having the option of staying tonight. You know, just in case. I'll keep trying my mate.

*PORTER enters.*

**PORTER:** Stand by your beds. It's OK. Not you, Frank.

**NURSE:** Can I help you?

**PORTER:** Now there's a leading question. About time isn't it? Lunch?

**NURSE:** Oh. Right.

**PORTER:** Or are you busy?

**NURSE:** No. I'll just go and make sure I've got cover.

**PORTER:** Don't bother on my account.

*NURSE exits. PORTER speaks to BRIAN.*

**PORTER:** Think I've embarrassed her. We are not supposed to fraternise in front of the patients.

**BRIAN:** You were hardly fraternising.

**PORTER:** Well, you know what I mean. You off then?

**BRIAN:** Not quite decided yet.

**PORTER:** You've not decided? Don't hang about, they might change their minds.

**FRANK:** Bollocks!

**PORTER:** Francis! Wash your mouth out.

**FRANK:** What?

*PORTER goes to FRANK.*

**PORTER:** You OK there mate? Were you sleeping?

**FRANK:** What?

**PORTER:** Or was your head in the clouds? That might explain the spherical objects.

**FRANK:** I don't know. I...

*FRANK is becoming distressed.*

**PORTER:** Listen, Frank. I just had this job to take a patient down to Discharge so I get there with the wheelchair and he's sat on the bed, fully dressed ready to go. I tell him to get in the wheelchair but he says he doesn't need it. But rules are rules so eventually he agreed. As we are going down in the lift I ask him if his wife is waiting for him in the Discharge Room and he says "No, I don't think so. She was still in the bathroom changing out of the hospital gown when we left".

*PORTER waits. Eventually FRANK chuckles.*

**PORTER:** Thought you'd like that one.

**BRIAN:** Has he been here long?

**PORTER:** Frank? About six months. Maybe more.

**BRIAN:** He was a headmaster, I believe.

**PORTER:** Don't know. I never concern myself with what people have been. It's what they are now that matters.

**BRIAN:** You are very good with him. Have you worked here long?

**PORTER:** Oh aye. I'm part of the furniture, me. I couldn't go back to my old job now. Not that there's any factories left anyway.

**BRIAN:** I suppose no two days are the same.

**PORTER:** Well, even if you're doing the same thing everyday it's the people that make it interesting. You see all sorts in here. Any colour, any class, any religion. Disease doesn't discriminate. The world and its arse comes through that door. You never know what's coming. Keeps you on your toes, I can tell you. We had that James Brown in here you know.

**BRIAN:** James Brown! Are you sure?

**PORTER:** Oh yes. He come in and he laid down the boogie and played that funky music till he died.

**BRIAN:** Very good.

**PORTER:** Glad you think so. My sense of humour gets me into more trouble than anything else.

**BRIAN:** You get a lot of satisfaction though.

**PORTER:** We have our moments I suppose. Speaking of which, the moment I've been waiting for all my life might be just about to happen. I'll go to see where her highness has got to. Um. Take care, mate. If I don't see you again. See you later, Frank.

*PORTER exits. BRIAN takes out his mobile phone and turns it on.*

*FRANK fidgets and hums to himself. BRIAN's phone beeps to indicate a message. He reads it, turns the phone off and packs his remaining bits into his bag. As he does so VICTORIA enters.*

**VICTORIA:** Dad!

**BRIAN:** Vic! What are you doing here?

**VICTORIA:** Jim rang.

**BRIAN:** Jim?

**VICTORIA:** You know. "Jim from the quiz team". Your new flat mate. Not.

**BRIAN:** I just had a text from him. He said to get a taxi.

**VICTORIA:** Check the time on the text, Dad. He rang after he sent it.

**BRIAN:** But why did he ring?

**VICTORIA:** To tell mum to stop being a twat.

**BRIAN:** What?

**VICTORIA:** I didn't think he had it in him.

**BRIAN:** He hardly knows your mum.

**VICTORIA:** Good job. I can't see him speaking to her like that otherwise.

**BRIAN:** And what did she say?

**VICTORIA:** What do you think she said? She told him to fuck off and mind his own business.

**BRIAN:** Right.

**VICTORIA:** So I told her that it was my business and if she wouldn't listen to him, she could fucking listen to me. There's more chance of you sprouting breasts and changing your name to Trixie than there is of you shagging another woman. She should know that.

**BRIAN:** Vic, it's more complicated than that. It isn't just this, it's been going on for years.

**VICTORIA:** What has?

**BRIAN:** We've been growing apart.

**VICTORIA:** Fuck sake, Dad. I've spent all morning persuading mum to let you come home. You go to Jim's and it's finished. The end. Come home and give it another try. Please.

**BRIAN:** We've talked about it...

**VICTORIA:** We haven't talked about it. You and mum have talked about it. I was never part of that discussion

**BRIAN:** But...

**VICTORIA:** Who do you love, Dad? Apart from me?

**BRIAN:** (*Eventually*) Your mother.

**VICTORIA:** Right, so come on.

**BRIAN:** Where is she?

**VICTORIA:** In the car.

**BRIAN:** She brought you?

**VICTORIA:** Yes! Haven't you been listening? We've come to take you home.

**BRIAN:** Why didn't she come up?

**VICTORIA:** Because she's too tight to pay four quid to park. She's sat in the pickup area with the engine running.

**BRIAN:** I just need to get my head round this.

**VICTORIA:** Get your head round it in the car. Mum's driving and don't you dare say a word to her about it. I'm not having an argument before we even get home.

**BRIAN:** But. Jim....

**VICTORIA:** Dad! There's nothing to think about. Come on. You're coming home.

**BRIAN:** OK, Vic. You're incredible, do you know that. I'll give it a go.

**VICTORIA:** Don't sound like you are doing me a favour. Few years from now I'll be gone to uni and all you two will have is each other, so you'd best do more than 'give it a go', you'd best make it work, OK?

**BRIAN:** I love you, Vic.

**VICTORIA:** Whatever. Yeah, Dad. I love you too. Come on.

*BRAIN and VICTORIA exit. FRANK fidgets.*

**FRANK:** (*Sings*) Breathe on me, breath of God, Fill me with life anew...
Clear off. I know you're there.
Buggers. Using my yard.
Clear off with your drugs.

**FRANK:** Taking advantage.
What? What have they done here? They've bloody glued all this.

*As FRANK sings the remainder of the hymn the lights fade and music fades in.*

**FRANK:** Breathe on me, Breath of God, until my heart is pure, until with thee I will one will, to do and to endure. Breathe on me, Breath of God, till I am wholly thine, till all this earthly part of me glows with thy fire divine. Breathe on me, Breath of God, so shall I never die, but live with thee the perfect life of thine eternity.

*END*

# OTHER PLAYS BY DAVID MUNCASTER

## Silvermoon Publishing
*www.silvermoonpublishing.co.uk*

The World and its Arse
I Gave You My Heart
Everyone's A Twinner

## New Theatre Publications
www.plays4theatre.com

Call Girls
Community Spirit
Fresh Flowers for the Thirsting Flowers
Mad Gary's Fruit and Nut Case
Mission Impossible
Waiting for a Train

## YouthPlays
*www.youthplays.com*

The Kennel Club

## Jasper Publications
*www.jasperpubllishing.com*

Life Begins at Seventy
Life Begins Again

# OTHER PLAYS PUBLISHED BY SILVERMOON PUBLISHING

**Nativity**
by Jonathan Hall
(2m, 3f)
It's December 1979 and class 2G are getting ready for the school Nativity. Gemma wants to be Mary but because she's got a big loud voice she's the narrator, and anyway Sarah her best friend is far loads prettier than her, everyone says so. And as for Kirsty- she doesn't even get a look in, not that she cares, she's bothered about showing her knickers in the practical area. And of course there can only be one choice for Joseph, and that'd have to be Tony, everyone's favourite, complete with his thirteen colour biro. And Nicholas? In love with Sarah and dreams of flying through the milky way with her in the TARDIS? He's always going to be the Innkeeper.

Nativity is about the play we've all been in. About tea towels on heads and coconut-shell donkey hooves. Dinner ladies and toilet roll angels, reading books and Blue Peter. It's about our six year old selves, the adults that shaped us, the dreams that lit our days- and the people we have become.

**I Gave You My Heart**
by David Muncaster
(2f)
Kate has received a parcel through the post from her ex-boyfriend. Her sister, Jenny thinks it is sweet, sending her a nice little parting gift. But Dan isn't sweet according to Kate. He's a freak a weirdo. And whatever is in that box is somehow related to the last thing that he wrote on Kate's Facebook page – "I gave you my heart"

**Flushed**
by Ron Nicol
(3f)
It's a singles night, and Jan and Meg are taking a break in the Ladies Room. Jan is criticising Tara, unaware that Tara is hiding in one of the toilet cubicles. When Tara's
presence is revealed a fight ensues and Jan confesses the reason for her jealousy. Then Meg discovers that the door to the room seems to be locked, and the succeeding series of mishaps and misfortunes ruins Jan's appearance and assurance. Tara eventually manages to open the door, but on the threshold of escape they find that Meg is trapped in one of the cubicles.

**A Beginner's Guide To Murdering Your Husband**
by David Muncaster
(3f,2m)
This play is presented as though it is an instructional video that the audience are watching being filmed. Maddy will present a variety of methods for disposing of an unwanted husband, aided by Jim, her real life husband, and her faithful employees. But is she really trying to get rid of her husband? Is the video just a ruse to lull him into a false sense of security? The parallels with their real life relationship give Jim plenty to worry about but, as the play reaches its its climax, we realise that nothing is what it seems. Criss-cross indeed!

# The only monthly magazine passionate about amateur theatre

**subscribe online:**
www.asmagazine.co.uk

Scan the QR Code to join us on Facebook

Follow us on twitter @amateurstage

www.ingramcontent.com/pod-product-compliance
Lightning Source LLC
Chambersburg PA
CBHW061506040426
42450CB00008B/1504

we once knew –simply because we're not spending the time in prayer before God that we once did? What was it that accounted for the weakness and disarray of the disciples in Gethsemane's garden?

Didn't our Lord make the answer clear, by repeatedly encouraging them to "watch and pray"? Their neglect of prayer was surely connected with their powerless performance. It's left on record for our learning. At the age of 86, John Wesley wrote these words in his journal, "Laziness is slowly creeping in. There is an increasing tendency to stay in bed after 5:30 in the morning." He was finding it harder and harder to get up at 5:30 a.m. for his daily devotions! Small wonder that this was a man with power in his ministry - John Wesley travelled 250,000 miles on horseback, preached 40,000 to 50,000 sermons, produced hundreds of pieces of literature, and at the age of 83 he was angry with his doctor because the doctor didn't let him preach more than fourteen times in a week!

To take another mighty example, it's also said that the sun never rose on China, but that it found pioneering missionary Hudson Taylor at prayer. His consistency and the store he set by prayer challenge us. By the grace of God these men left their mark on history – and our intention here is not to give glory to the instrument, but to acknowledge the God they glorified through such prayerful lives. James, in his Bible book, gives it to us straight when he explains that the prayer of a righteous person has great power – it's effective and accomplishes much (James 5:16). He used Elijah as his biblical example. Elijah's prayer – which was according to God's Word, and that fact must be stressed – stopped all rainfall for three-and-a-half years, until he prayed again, and this time for the rain which then came (see 1 Kings 17:1; 18:1). Talk about the powerful ministry of a right-living man through prayer! The power and spirit of Elijah became proverbial (Luke 1:17)!

Now James actually precedes that comment on prayer with the mention of the confession of sins. This was also something which we've seen was a feature of Daniel's prayer. As a prayer intercessor, he identified with the sins of the people for whom he was praying. So with that link of confession in mind, we come to Matthew 18 where we read in verse 19: "... if two of you agree on earth about anything they ask, it will be done for them by my Father in heaven." What's the connection, you may ask? Well, this is two or three agreeing together to ask in prayer immediately after forgiveness and agreement have been expressed between them. The context is one where some offence has been given, and the offended party has taken a couple of witnesses in the hope of resolving the matter with the brother concerned who was the instigator.

We first read the details in verse 17 of the procedure to be followed when a satisfactory outcome isn't reached; and then in verse 19 of what happens in the happier case when agreement is reached and harmony restored. In that case, in accord with God's Word – and here it's the personal counsel of our Lord – when we agree to bury any dispute and genuinely ask God to help us make it stick, then that's a prayer God will answer positively, for sure. Lying underneath our real need for improved relationships; for more purity; less greed; greater evangelical fervour; and for deeper Bible study: there lies our primary, fundamental need for powerfully transformed lives by knowing God better through transformed praying.

# CHAPTER TWO: COMPROMISE YOUR SEPARATION TO GOD

So far, we've thought about the loss of spiritual power in serving God which comes about when we neglect prayer or neglect meditating on God's Word, the Bible. Sometimes we can still go through the motions of prayer and reading, but prayer has already become perfunctory and our reading dry and disinterested. Our passion for the things of God has dried up, and God no longer seems close, or even real in our lives, and God's power through us no longer blesses others as it once did.

One of the strangest and saddest stories in Old Testament history is the story of Samson. It's also one of the most instructive. He was by far the most remarkable man of his day. The greatest opportunities were open to him, but after making some victorious progress, his life ended in tragic failure – and all through his own inexcusable folly. Here's how it happened:

> "... it came about that he loved a woman in the valley of Sorek, whose name was Delilah. The lords of the Philistines came up to her and said to her, "Entice him, and see where his great strength lies and how we may overpower him that we may bind him to afflict him. Then we will each give you eleven hundred pieces of silver."
>
> So Delilah said to Samson, "Please tell me where your great strength is and how you may be bound to afflict you." ... It came about when she pressed him daily

with her words and urged him, that his soul was annoyed to death. So he told her all that was in his heart and said to her, "A razor has never come on my head, for I have been a Nazirite to God from my mother's womb. If I am shaved, then my strength will leave me and I will become weak and be like any other man." When Delilah saw that he had told her all that was in his heart, she sent and called the lords of the Philistines, saying, "Come up, once more, for he has told me all that is in his heart."

Then the lords of the Philistines came up to her and brought the money in their hands. She made him sleep on her knees, and called for a man and had him shave off the seven locks of his hair. Then she began to afflict him, and his strength left him" (Judges 16:4-19).

Notice the outcome: his strength left him. That says it all. Before this, time and again it had been said of him that the Spirit of the Lord had come mightily upon him, and in that power he had acted in such powerful ways that he'd astonished his own people and wasted the enemies of the Lord. But when we get to this point, we find him deserted by the Lord, although at first he's unaware this has happened. Along with his hair, his separation to God and his strength have gone – and he's about to be taken captive by the enemy, to be mocked and abused by the godless Philistines. Unfortunately, Samson isn't the only one in either biblical or Christian history, who, having once known the power of the Holy Spirit, has afterward been shorn of this same power. There have been many Samsons – those whom God once used – but afterwards had to lay aside.

Why? What lesson can we learn from this about the loss of spiritual power? Well, from Samson, we learn that God withdraws his power when we go back on our separation to him (Judges 16:19. Compare Numbers 6:2,5). Samson's uncut hair was the outward sign of his Nazirite vow by which he had separated or dedicated himself to the Lord. The shearing of that hair – which was meant to be left uncut for as long as the vow lasted – would equally then seem to symbolize something.

If letting his hair grow uncut was the symbol of his vow of dedicated separation to God, it stands to reason that the cutting of that same hair would symbolize the surrender of that same separation: that his period of dedication was now at an end. And with his separation surrendered, we see from Samson's example that he was also shorn of his power. In the same way we, too, can be shorn of power. There was a day when we separated ourselves to God, was there not? We may have sung at our baptism: 'The cross before me; the world behind me.'

We turned our backs on the world and its ambitions. We set ourselves apart to God, committed ourselves to his service, and often with a passionate spirituality. We gave ourselves unreservedly so that God could take us and use us for whatever he wanted. God honoured this separation and dedication. And for a while we were used by God, perhaps even powerfully used. But then the world – like Delilah – came to us and captured our heart once again. We listened to its siren voice and allowed it to shear us of our separation and power. We became no longer wholly consecrated to the Lord. There's an old hymn which says:

"O Jesus, I have promised

To serve Thee to the end;

Be Thou forever near me

My Master and my Friend;

I shall not fear the battle

If Thou art by my side,

Nor wander from the pathway

If Thou wilt be my Guide.


O let me feel Thee near me!

The world is ever near;

I see the sights that dazzle,

The tempting sounds I hear;

My foes are ever near me

Around me and within;

But Jesus, draw Thou nearer,

And shield my soul from sin."

John Bode wrote these original words for his daughter and two sons to aspire to. Did we not once make them our personal vow? We may still sing them with enthusiasm. But do they still reflect our heart's devotion? Is it true of us? Or is it true that we've once been used by the Lord and yet he doesn't use us so much nowadays? We may still be in Christian work, but there's not the liberty and power in it that there once was – and this is the reason: we've got casual in the matter of our separation, and our consecration to God. Why? Because we've been listening to our Delilah, that is to this attractive world with all its tempting attractions.

Samson loved Delilah, and he paid dearly for that love. If we can think of the world in these terms as our Delilah – as something that comes between us and the Lord and draws away our heart devotion from Christ – then the Apostle John's words seem very relevant and strong in their appeal:

> "I have written to you, young men, because you are strong, and the word of God abides in you, and you have overcome the evil one. Do not love the world nor the things in the world. If anyone loves the world, the love of the Father is not in him. For all that is in the world, the lust of the flesh and the lust of the eyes and the boastful pride of life, is not from the Father, but is from the world. The world is passing away, and also its lusts; but the one who does the will of God lives forever" (1 John 2:15-17).

How much Samson could have used a warning as clear as that, but he was switched off, sleeping in the arms of his lover, oblivious to the danger he was in. The chilling thing is we could be in a similar position: cosying up to the world, enjoying its charms. It feels good, we think we have it all under control, but we're paying the price of spiritual weakness and ineffectiveness. Do we want that old power back again? If so, there's only one thing to do: we need to renew our consecration to God. As when Paul writes in Romans:

> "Therefore I urge you, brethren, by the mercies of God, to present your bodies a living and holy sacrifice, acceptable to God, which is your spiritual service of worship. And do not be conformed to this world, but be transformed by the renewing of your mind, so that you may prove what the will of God is, that which is good and acceptable and perfect" (Romans 12:1-2).

We're in the world, but the problem is that the world gets into us. It's always trying to squeeze us into its mould. And that's very different from the mould or pattern of Christ's teaching which is meant to be the thing that shapes us (Romans 6:17). Even as he stepped towards the cross, Christ prayed for us like this in John 17: "They are not of the world, even as I am not of the world. Sanctify them in the truth; Your word is truth ... For their sakes I sanctify Myself, that they themselves also may be sanctified in truth" (John 17:16-19).

Do we feel the Spirit of the Saviour tugging at our heart? Makes us want to be sanctified – to be separated again, doesn't it? Perhaps we can make use of an Old Testament incident as an illustration of the way to recover power. It's set in the days of Elisha:

> "So he went with them; and when they came to the Jordan, they cut down trees. But as one was felling a beam, the axe head fell into the water; and he cried out and said, "Alas, my master! For it was borrowed." Then the man of God said, "Where did it fall?" And when he showed him the place, he cut off a stick and threw it in there, and made the iron float. He said, "Take it up for yourself." So he put out his hand and took it" (2 Kings 6:4-7).

In a literal sense that man had lost the cutting edge in his service! He was no longer as effective without it. Elisha advised him how to get it back by returning to the spot where he'd lost it. If we sense we've lost our power in service, our cutting edge, so to speak, we need to ask the Lord's help to take us back to where we lost it. And perhaps that's the crux of the matter in this chapter: pinpointing the loss as due to a slackness that's crept into our devotion, a distance that's intruded into our walk with the Lord, all because we've let the attractive world steal into our hearts. If so, we now know what to do, don't we?

# CHAPTER THREE: LET SIN ENTER YOUR LIFE

Perhaps the most obvious cause of the loss of spiritual power in our lives is sinful behaviour. But we need to think about what exactly we mean by that. I'm impressed by the answer that Suzannah Wesley once gave her son John when he asked her, "Can you give me a definition for sin?" She said: "Whatever weakens your reasoning, impairs the tenderness of your conscience, obscures your sense of God, or takes away your relish for spiritual things, in short if anything increases the authority and the power of the flesh over the spirit, that to you becomes sin, however good it is in itself."

What a thoughtful answer, probably extending well beyond our usual boundaries of meaning whenever we've tried to define sin! There was a woman who was seemingly intent on pleasing the Lord. A godly mother, whose influence shaped such children as John the preacher and Charles the hymn-writer. It's long struck me as remarkable how, in introducing kings, the Bible often mentions the new king's mother. Perhaps that, too, bears witness to the impact of a mother on her offspring. But returning to our point about sin: power goes out when sin comes in. And the biblical example I'd like to use concerns much more blatant sin than we've thought about earlier. As we said: power goes out when sin comes in. That's how it was with Saul, the son of Kish, the very first king of Israel. At the beginning of his reign, he was a man whom God used powerfully.

The Spirit of God came upon Saul and he won a great victory for God (1 Samuel 11:6). He brought the people to a place of triumph over the enemies who had controlled them for years. But then:

> "... the Philistines assembled to fight with Israel ... the men of Israel saw that they were in a strait (for the people were hard-pressed), then the people hid themselves in caves, in thickets, in cliffs, in cellars, and in pits. Also some of the Hebrews crossed the Jordan into the land of Gad and Gilead. But as for Saul, he was still in Gilgal, and all the people followed him trembling. Now he waited seven days, according to the appointed time set by Samuel, but Samuel did not come to Gilgal; and the people were scattering from him. So Saul said, "Bring to me the burnt offering and the peace offerings." And he offered the burnt offering. As soon as he finished offering the burnt offering, behold, Samuel came; and Saul went out to meet him and to greet him. But Samuel said, "What have you done?" And Saul said, "Because I saw that the people were scattering from me, and that you did not come within the appointed days, and that the Philistines were assembling at Michmash, therefore I said, 'Now the Philistines will come down against me at Gilgal, and I have not asked the favor of the LORD.' So I forced myself and offered the burnt offering." Samuel said to Saul, "You have acted foolishly; you have not kept the commandment of the LORD your God, which He commanded you,

for now the LORD would have established your kingdom over Israel forever. But now your kingdom shall not endure" (1 Samuel 13:5-14).

This was the first of two distinct instances in which Saul disobeyed the Lord. The other is found two chapters later in 1 Samuel 15:

> "Thus says the LORD of hosts, 'I will punish Amalek for what he did to Israel, how he set himself against him on the way while he was coming up from Egypt. Now go and strike Amalek and utterly destroy all that he has, and do not spare him; but put to death both man and woman, child and infant, ox and sheep, camel and donkey.'" ... Saul came to the city of Amalek and set an ambush in the valley ... So Saul defeated the Amalekites, from Havilah as you go to Shur, which is east of Egypt. He captured Agag the king of the Amalekites alive, and utterly destroyed all the people with the edge of the sword. But Saul and the people spared Agag and the best of the sheep, the oxen, the fatlings, the lambs, and all that was good, and were not willing to destroy them utterly; but everything despised and worthless, that they utterly destroyed. Then the word of the LORD came to Samuel, saying, "I regret that I have made Saul king, for he has turned back from following Me and has not carried out My commands" (1 Samuel 15:2-11).

With that second act of sinful disobedience by Saul, the Lord withdrew his favour and power, and Saul's life ended in utter defeat and ruin. His career as king, which had begun one memorable sunrise, ended in a murky sunset as the sun went down on Mount Gilboa. Saul's sin, his disobeying God, his carelessness in carrying out the Word of God, had cost him the sustained privilege of the experience of God's power in his life. And this is the shared history of many others whom God has once used, and then sin has crept in. Perhaps there are times we've known it too: when we've done what God told us not to, or we've refused to do what God commanded, and the power of God that we once felt has been withdrawn. Of course, there's a sense in which we're always struggling with this – all of us – just as we find the apostle Paul saying in Romans 7:16: "I am not practising what I would like to do, but I am doing the very thing I hate …"

This is the chapter of the Romans letter in which Paul writes about indwelling sin before, in the very next chapter, writing instead about the indwelling Holy Spirit and his power in our lives, helping us to overcome the power of sin. If we want to prolong any spiritual power we've known we should make it our ambition to live according to the Spirit. It's interesting to note that in chapter 8 of Romans, the apostle Paul makes a difference between those who are 'in the flesh' and those who are 'in the Spirit'. By these two categories, he means unbelievers (who are in the flesh); and by contrast believers (who are in the Spirit) – where the reference is to the Holy Spirit. Then he also distinguishes between those who are living 'according to the flesh' and those who are living 'according to the Spirit.' In this case, he's contrasting lifestyles. Sadly, then, it's possible to be a Christian believer (someone who's in the Spirit) and yet still be living 'according to the flesh.'

So, that's why we need to daily ask the Lord to show us if any sin, anything displeasing in his sight, has crept in that day, and then confess it and put it away there and then. In other words, we claim the provision of 1 John 1:9: "If we confess our sins, He is faithful and righteous to forgive us our sins and to cleanse us from all unrighteousness." But clearly there are more serious sins with fatal consequences for our lives of service for God. When we get to the fifth chapter of John's first letter, we're told:

> "If anyone sees his brother committing a sin not leading to death, he shall ask and God will ... give life to those who commit sin not leading to death. There is a sin leading to death; I do not say that he should make request for this. All unrighteousness is sin, and there is a sin not leading to death" (1 John 5:16-17).

There's a category of sinning being referred to here which is terminal as far as any future life of productive service for God is concerned down here. John doesn't identify it for us – although the preceding context of the letter has largely been taken up with a discussion of anti-Christian beliefs and attitudes which we need to oppose and, of course, steer personally clear of. Whether someone committing a sin leading to death – to use John's words – could be someone who had become sucked into that kind of major doctrinal error – one which impacted on core Christian beliefs like the incarnation and the atonement isn't made explicit.

But surely that's an example of something that would qualify. For if the preaching of the cross is made void of power, if it's emptied of its power, then it's simply impossible that there could be spiritual power in that preacher's ministry. So sin – disobedience to God's Word – might be behavioural or it might be doctrinal. What's very clear is this: that someone who has known God's power in service and wants to continue to know it, must walk very softly before him – obeying God's voice in the Word.

# CHAPTER FOUR: BE PROUD

In this chapter, we're going to look at a couple of powerful men – spiritual giants, but ones who lost their power. Their case studies will help us as we continue to identify the most common reasons for how spiritual power can be lost in our lives. The first of these men is Uzziah. He was a godly king who reigned in Jerusalem over the two southern tribes of Israel. His story occupies 2 Chronicles 26. God rewarded Uzziah's godliness by giving him success in several areas of his life, including in his military adventures by means of which he destroyed Philistine towns. He was also successful in campaigns against the Arabs; the Ammonites recognized his sovereignty over them, and his fame spread as far as Egypt's borders.

Uzziah also masterminded the construction of fortress towers in Jerusalem at various points on Jerusalem's walls. He was involved in massive agricultural projects in the desert as well as in the foothills and plains. He reorganized an army of over 300,000 men into well-trained and well-equipped divisions, and pioneered the use of certain advanced weapons like catapults which launched arrows and large stones. All this enhanced his reputation and increased his strength. But then we read: "His fame spread afar, for he was marvellously helped until he was strong. But when he became strong, his heart was so proud that he acted corruptly, and he was unfaithful to the LORD his God, for he entered the temple of the LORD to burn incense on the altar of incense" (2 Chronicles 26:16).

Uzziah's power led to pride, and this proved to be his downfall (see Proverbs 16:18; 18:12). Apparently, he had begun to depend on his armies and weapons rather than on the LORD. He even presumed to offer incense in the temple, a sacrilege for which the priests roundly condemned him. For the king to attempt to do this meant that he was being unfaithful to the Law of God (2 Chronicles 26:16-18), which restricted the burning of incense to priests only (Exodus 30:7-8). Uzziah responded in rage, but the action of the priests in preventing the king from burning incense was shown to be right when leprosy broke out on the king's forehead. God had judged King Uzziah. A couple of chapters later in 2 Chronicles, we find our second example of a powerful servant of God whose life was spoiled. King Hezekiah was another good man through whom God did great things – but whose service was brought to an end like Uzziah's for the same reason: because he also became proud. Once again Hezekiah began well:

> "Hezekiah became king when he was twenty-five years old; and he reigned twenty-nine years in Jerusalem. And his mother's name was Abijah, the daughter of Zechariah. He did right in the sight of the LORD, according to all that his father David had done. In the first year of his reign, in the first month, he opened the doors of the house of the LORD and repaired them. He brought in the priests and the Levites and gathered them into the square on the east. Then he said to them, "Listen to me, O Levites.

Consecrate yourselves now, and consecrate the house of the LORD, the God of your fathers, and carry the uncleanness out from the holy place ...

Thus the service of the house of the LORD was established again ... So there was great joy in Jerusalem, because there was nothing like this in Jerusalem since the days of Solomon the son of David, king of Israel ... Hezekiah ... did what was good, right and true before the LORD his God. Every work which he began in the service of the house of God in law and in commandment, seeking his God, he did with all his heart and prospered ... And many were bringing gifts to the LORD at Jerusalem and choice presents to Hezekiah king of Judah, so that he was exalted in the sight of all nations thereafter" (2 Chronicles 29:1-23).

What a wonderful life-story! Glory to God! We can see real spiritual power in King Hezekiah's life which accomplished so much for the Lord. It would have been good if it had ended there. But sadly there's a postscript: "Hezekiah became mortally ill; and he prayed to the LORD, and the LORD spoke to him and gave him a sign" (2 Chronicles 32:24). In fact, God answered King Hezekiah's prayer, and he recovered and was granted a fifteen-year extension to his life. But sadly, we now continue to read from the Bible record: "But Hezekiah gave no return for the benefit he received, because his heart was proud" (v.25) ... and then as if to explain how that pride had come about, the Bible historian says:

"Now Hezekiah had immense riches and honor; and he made for himself treasuries for silver, gold, precious stones, spices, shields and all kinds of valuable articles, storehouses also for the produce of grain, wine and oil, pens for all kinds of cattle and sheepfolds for the flocks. He made cities for himself and acquired flocks and herds in abundance, for God had given him very great wealth. It was Hezekiah who stopped the upper outlet of the waters of Gihon and directed them to the west side of the city of David. And Hezekiah prospered in all that he did. Even in the matter of the envoys of the rulers of Babylon, who sent to him to inquire of the wonder that had happened in the land, God left him alone only to test him, that He might know all that was in his heart" (2 Chronicles 32:27-31).

These final verses describing Hezekiah seem to catalogue the accomplishments which became the reason for the pride for which he was judged. He had wealth and honour; he built storage facilities, agricultural settlements, and villages; he rerouted the city's water supply from the Gihon spring (in the Kidron Valley on the east) to the west side, and succeeded in these and many other undertakings. The tunnel of Hezekiah was dug through solid rock from the Gihon spring to the Pool of Siloam, a distance of more than 500 metres with workmen digging from each end and meeting in the middle – a significant accomplishment. But then we read of how foolishly and proudly he displayed all the wealth of the temple and his palace to his Babylonian neighbours (2 Kings 20:12-19; Isaiah 39:1).

The narrator then simply says that God allowed all this to test him and to know everything that was in his heart. That is, God wanted to show Hezekiah himself the consequences of pride. And he wanted to show it to us, too. Power is lost through pride. It's the subtlest and most dangerous of all the enemies of power. Hezekiah is an example of someone who didn't consciously go back upon his consecration, as Samson had done. Nor did he nurture sin in the sense of obviously doing what God prohibited – as Saul had done – but yet he still failed because pride came in. He became puffed up just because of the very fact that God had given him power and used him in the first place. God – the God who resists the proud and gives grace to the humble (1 Peter 5:5) was forced to set him aside.

Today, the person who's puffed up with pride and self-confidence cannot be filled with the Holy Spirit. Paul saw this danger for himself, after God saw it for him first, and he could say: "... to keep me from exalting myself, there was given me a thorn in the flesh, a messenger of Satan to torment me – to keep me from exalting myself!" (2 Corinthians 12:7). We'd do well to learn from Paul. Many – like Uzziah and Hezekiah – have looked for God's power in God's way, and it's come. Others have testified of the blessing received through their ministry, but in the end pride has entered in. If God is using us at all, let us get down very low before him. The more he uses us, the lower we need to get. For God says: "But to this one I will look, to him who is humble and contrite of spirit, and who trembles at My word" (Isaiah 66:2).

# CHAPTER FIVE: BE SELF-INDULGENT

The missionary Hudson Taylor once said: "An easy-going non-self-denying life will never be one of power" (A.J. Broomhall. Hudson Taylor and China's Open Century, Book Six: Assault on the Nine London: Hodder and Stoughton and Overseas Missionary Fellowship,1988, p.310.) As we go deeper in our study of the things to avoid if we're to be channels of God's power, we will now evaluate that claim by Hudson Taylor: that power is lost through self-indulgence. We'll find that it's biblical that the person who wants to know God's power in his or her service for God must lead a life of self- denial. The Lord said as much in Luke 9:23, when he said that those who came after him must deny themselves and take up their cross and so follow him.

R.A. Torrey – whose headings we've been following in this book – once said, 'I do not believe that any man can lead a luxurious life, overindulge his natural appetites, indulge extensively in dainties, AND enjoy the fullness of God's power.' It's certainly true that the gratification of the flesh and the fullness of the Spirit don't go hand in hand. Far from it, for Galatians 5:17 says: "The flesh sets its desire [or lusts] against the Spirit, and the Spirit against the flesh." We live in a day when the temptation to indulge the flesh is really strong because, in the west at least, luxuries are common and opportunities are plentiful. Piety and prosperity don't often go hand in hand. Jesus said, when talking about John the Baptist, that "those who wear soft clothing are in kings' palaces!" (Matthew 11:8). Those words didn't describe

John – he knew the king's prison, but not the king's palace! This is very different from popular preachers in today's celebrity culture where luxurious living and 'soft clothing' have come in, and the power of the Spirit has all too often gone out.

I've been reminded today of the Holy Spirit's description of Jacob as a "plain man". A modern Christian song about the Lord's challenging words to the rich young ruler is entitled 'simple living'. To experience the ongoing power of the Spirit in our service for God, we need to be on guard to lead lives of simplicity, free from indulgence and excess, ready to "endure hardship, as a good soldier of Jesus Christ" (2 Timothy 2:3). One of the most haunting passages among Paul's biblical letters, is found in 2 Timothy 4:10 where he writes: "Demas has forsaken me, having loved this present world, and has departed for Thessalonica."

The apostle Paul was a 'people person'. He ministered to people, he trained people, and, if you study his prayers, you'll notice he prayed for people – a lot. When one of those people, into whom he'd poured his life, turned back and deserted him, he must have really felt it. This sense of desolation seems to be reflected in the next verse when he wrote, "Only Luke is with me" (4:11). We're not told where Demas was from. Some think that, because he went to Thessalonica, it implies he was returning to his hometown. If Demas was from Thessalonica, it would be interesting to compare his life with that of Aristarchus who was also from Thessalonica. Both may have been from a comfortable background and probably had some wealth, both were trained by the Apostle Paul, yet both men went in different spiritual directions.

Demas first appears in the Bible when he was in Rome during the Apostle Paul's first imprisonment (AD 60-62). In the last chapter of Colossians there's mention of at least eight believers, including Demas, who were there with Paul at that time – and all of whom were known to the churches in the Lycus Valley. Because of this, it would seem that Demas was a visiting missionary to the Lycus Valley at one time. Six of them send their greetings (Colossians 4:10-14), and Demas is listed with Dr. Luke and Epaphras (4:12-14), where they are set in contrast with the three Jewish believers, Aristarchus, Mark, and Justus (4:10-11). So this could mean that Demas was a Gentile. Five of Paul's companions, again including Demas, also send their personal greetings to Philemon at Colossae as well (Philemon vv.23-24). Among the greetings to Philemon, Demas is included in the statement that tells us he's a co-worker with Paul (Philemon 24). Perhaps he was a 'close confidant of Paul, sharing the Apostle's vision of winning the world for God' (W.D. Thomas, 1983-84: p.179).

All this would suggest he was someone who had been a channel of God's power and blessing to others in his mission work alongside Paul. But he had lost that power. Paul wrote that Demas 'forsook him' (2 Timothy 4:10). He had let Paul down. Why? Because he 'loved this present world'. Paul doesn't tell us which aspect of the present world system Demas loved. He doesn't say if it was fame, fortune, or the gratification of the flesh. Perhaps, he didn't want to embarrass his co-worker any further. But also leaving this failure in Demas' life unspecified in this way meant it could serve as a broad, general warning to us. And we all need that warning – for remember how the Apostle John wrote to believers in Asia Minor: "Do not love the world or the things of the world ... For all that is in the world – the lust of the flesh, the lust of the eyes, and the pride of life – is not of the Father but is of the world." (1 John 2:15-17).

The questions this raises are: "Are we living for time, or for eternity?" and, "Are we living for this world, or for God's kingdom?" The Christian should view the 'world' as often used in the New Testament, as a moral and spiritual system, which is designed to draw the believer in the Lord Jesus away from love for the Lord and any service for him (Galatians 1:4; 1 Timothy 6:17; Titus 2:12). The world in its cultures, beliefs and values tries to draw the believer away from his or her love for the Lord in one of three ways. The first, the lust of the flesh, has to do with what makes us feel good physically. It includes sexual sins, gluttony, drug use and drunkenness. The second way is the lust of the eyes (whatever we see that we want to possess) – when the object we want is not ours, but belongs to someone else, this comes down to covetousness.

And the final category is the pride of life (what we want to be) – boasting about our potential accomplishments. Whatever Demas' love for the world was, it almost certainly fell into at least one of these three categories. In the previous chapter we looked at pride and in the next we'll consider the topic of greed. Right now, we're wondering whether Demas' issue was more about desiring an easier lifestyle with more physical creature comforts. Why Demas went to Thessalonica, and what he did there isn't revealed in the Bible. One preacher who lived about AD 400 (John Chrysostom) suggested that 'having loved his own ease and security from danger, [Demas] had chosen rather to live luxuriously at home, than to suffer hardships' with Paul (quoted in Oden 1989: p.176). If this is the case, the allurement that Demas fell for was the lust of the flesh because he wanted an easy-going life with no self-denial.

Polycarp in the 2nd century A.D, wrote a letter in which he listed some early martyrs: Ignatius, Zosimus, Rufus, Paul and other apostles, and said that all these had not "run in vain" because they didn't "love this present world" (Polycarp to the Philippians 9:1-2; LCL I: 295). Polycarp seems to be contrasting them to Demas when he says they didn't love this present world. It seems that he is implying that Demas didn't want to be a martyr so that's why he abandoned Paul in Rome before he was executed. Certainly, just before Paul's statement about Demas abandoning him, he was talking about his own impending martyrdom (2 Timothy 4:6-8). Whether or not Demas was running away from hardship and martyrdom, or just wanting more creature comforts, an easier- going life, with a bit of indulgence and luxury thrown in; it's clear we shouldn't emulate the life of Demas. Instead, we should have an eternal perspective on life and not love this present world system that's out to draw us away from our devotion to the Lord and his Word.

The hope of the Lord's return should change the way we live now. Paul, in contrast to Demas, lived his life in the light of the judgement-seat of Christ. Certainly, none of us is immune from loving this present world and leaving the Lord's work and the Lord's people (1 Corinthians 10:12). We've seen that the allurement of this world falls into three categories, but neither do we have to fail! The Lord Jesus, as the perfect man, was tested in these ways, and passed the tests with flying colours because he was filled with the Spirit and used the Word of God when Satan attacked. These same resources are available to us.

# CHAPTER SIX: BE GREEDY

In his book, I Talk Back to the Devil, the Christian author A.W. Tozer reminds us of the fact that: 'Money often comes between us and God. Someone has said that you can take two small [coins] and shut out the view of a panoramic landscape. Go to the mountains and just hold two coins closely in front of your eyes – the mountains are still there, but you cannot see them at all ... It doesn't take large quantities of money to come between us and God; just a little, placed in the wrong position, will effectively obscure our view.' In Luke's Gospel, chapter 12, we find the following incident narrated:

> "One day ... someone in the crowd said to [Jesus], "Teacher, tell my brother to divide the family inheritance with me." But He said to him, "... be on your guard against every form of greed ..." (Luke 12:13-14).

The person who has known God's power working through them is not immune to the desire to become rich. The apostle Paul sounded this warning to Timothy, as he explained to him that:

> "... godliness actually is a means of great gain when accompanied by contentment. For we have brought nothing into the world, so we cannot take anything out of it either. If we have food and covering, with these we shall be content. But those who want to get rich fall into temptation and a snare and many foolish and harmful desires which plunge men into ruin and

destruction. For the love of money is a root of all sorts of evil, and some by longing for it have wandered away from the faith and pierced themselves with many griefs. But flee from these things, you man of God, and pursue righteousness, godliness, faith, love, perseverance and gentleness. Fight the good fight of faith; take hold of the eternal life to which you were called, and you made the good confession in the presence of many witnesses" (1 Timothy 6:6-12).

Perhaps the desire to get rich and the love of money played a major role in the lives of two early disciples in the first churches of God. Their names were Ananias and Sapphira. We read about them in Acts chapter 5:

"But a man named Ananias, with his wife Sapphira, sold a piece of property, and kept back some of the price for himself, with his wife's full knowledge, and bringing a portion of it, he laid it at the apostles' feet. But Peter said, "Ananias, why has Satan filled your heart to lie to the Holy Spirit and to keep back some of the price of the land? While it remained unsold, did it not remain your own? And after it was sold, was it not under your control? Why is it that you have conceived this deed in your heart? You have not lied to men but to God." And as he heard these words, Ananias fell down and breathed his last; and great fear came over all who heard of it. The young men got up and covered him up, and after carrying him out, they buried him. Now there elapsed an interval of about three hours, and his wife came in, not knowing what had happened.

And Peter responded to her, "Tell me whether you sold the land for such and such a price?" And she said, "Yes, that was the price." Then Peter said to her, "Why is it that you have agreed together to put the Spirit of the Lord to the test? Behold, the feet of those who have buried your husband are at the door, and they will carry you out as well." And immediately she fell at his feet and breathed her last, and the young men came in and found her dead, and they carried her out and buried her beside her husband. And great fear came over the whole church, and over all who heard of these things" (Acts 5:1-11).

As well as wanting to impress people with their generosity, their hearts were controlled by greed in what they secretly kept back for themselves. Someone has said, 'There are two ways in which a Christian may view his money and his giving – [either] "How much of my money shall I use for God?" Or "How much of God's money shall I use for myself?" (W. Graham Scroggie). I'm sure you get the point. It's the same money. It's the money in my pocket and in my bank and in my possessions – but it's a question of my attitude to it: do I consider it as my money or God's money which I have on trust to use wisely. Instead of having the second outlook of 'How much of God's money shall I use for myself?'; Ananias and his wife operated out of the first point of view: 'How much of my money shall I use for God?'

As we saw earlier, Paul was in effect commending the second mindset to Timothy: that is, 'How much of God's money shall I use for myself?'

You remember that he said: "... godliness actually is a means of great gain when accompanied by contentment. For we have brought nothing into the world, so we cannot take anything out of it either. If we have food and covering, with these we shall be content. But those who want to get rich fall into temptation and a snare and many foolish and harmful desires which plunge men into ruin and destruction. For the love of money is a root of all sorts of evil, and some by longing for it have wandered away from the faith and pierced themselves with many griefs" (1 Timothy 6:6-10).

In other words, what the Apostle Paul everywhere advocates is the mindset which says, 'all that I have is the Lord's and not my own' and so with modest provision for my needs and those of my family I should be content. Even when our motives are not as impure as those of Ananias, Paul saw the potential danger and made this point to the recent converts at Thessalonica as he reminded them of his time spent preaching among them:

> "For our exhortation does not come from error or impurity or by way of deceit; but just as we have been approved by God to be entrusted with the gospel, so we speak, not as pleasing men, but God who examines our hearts. For we never came with flattering speech, as you know, nor with a pretext for greed ..." (1 Thessalonians 2:3-5).

There's no doubt about it: power is lost through greed for money. It was through this that a member of the original apostolic company, the chosen twelve, fell. The love of money, the love of accumulation or getting more, got into the heart of Judas Iscariot, and it proved to be the means of his downfall. "The love of money is a root of all evil" (1 Timothy 6:10), and certainly one evil of which it is a root is the loss of spiritual power. There have been people down through the years who once knew what spiritual power was, but then money began to come, and they felt its strange fascination. The love for more, little by little took possession of them. It was all accumulated honestly; but still it absorbed them, and in due course power departed.

As servants of Christ, we need to have his words, "... be on your guard against every form of greed ..." (Luke 12:15), engraved on our hearts. A person doesn't even need to be rich in order to be covetous or greedy. In fact, a very poor person may be as much absorbed in the desire for wealth as a rich man – or even more so, out of desperation.

# CHAPTER SEVEN: INVALIDATE GOD'S WORD

The famous Scottish minister, James Stewart, who preached at Edinburgh, Scotland, penned the following words in a book written for preachers which he entitled: "Heralds of God":

"Surely there are few figures so pitiable as the disillusioned minister of the Gospel. High hopes cheered him on his way, but now the indifference and the recalcitrance of the world, the lack of strikingly visible results, the discovery of appalling pettiness and spite and touchiness and complacency which can lodge in narrow hearts, the feeling of personal futility, all these have seared his soul. No longer does the zeal of God's house devour him. No longer does he mount the pulpit steps in thrilled expectancy that Jesus Christ will come amongst his folk that day travelling in the greatness of his strength, mighty to save. Dully and drearily, he speaks now about what seemed once to him the most dramatic tidings in the world.

The edge and verve and passion of the message of divine forgiveness, the exultant, lyrical, assurance of the presence of the risen Lord, the amazement of supernatural grace, the urge to cry, "Woe is me if I preach not the gospel" - all have suddenly gone. The man has lost heart. He is disillusioned and that for an ambassador of Christ is a tragedy."

And not only a tragedy for himself, but surely his disillusioned demeanour can only serve to seemingly invalidate for others the vibrant message he once so brightly expressed. The religious leaders - the teachers of God's Word - known in Jesus' day as the scribes and Pharisees, had certainly lost their way in God's Word. Although let's be clear that they never, at any time, had known the joy in the Word which James Stewart speaks about. That much, at least, is clear from what we find recorded at the beginning of Matthew's Gospel, chapter 15:

> "Then some Pharisees and scribes came to Jesus from Jerusalem and said, "Why do Your disciples break the tradition of the elders? For they do not wash their hands when they eat bread." And He answered and said to them, "Why do you yourselves transgress the commandment of God for the sake of your tradition? For God said, 'Honor your father and mother,' and, 'He who speaks evil of father or mother is to be put to death.' But you say, 'Whoever says to his father or mother, "Whatever I have that would help you has been given to God," he is not to honor his father or his mother.' And by this you invalidated the word of God for the sake of your tradition. You hypocrites, rightly did Isaiah prophesy of you: 'This people honor me with their lips, but their heart is far away from me. But in vain do they worship me, teaching as doctrines the precepts of men'" (Matthew 15:1-9).

Notice what was happening here. The Jewish teachers were criticising Jesus' disciples for failing to keep their own time-honoured Jewish traditions. But Jesus had no sympathy with this accusation against his followers. He rather says to the accusers in effect: "I want you to tell me why you prefer to maintain your traditions at the expense of God's plain commands found in his Word." The mistake these Jewish leaders were making has been made many times since. It's a long-standing feature of religious history down through the ages, right to the present time. Straightforward Bible commands are set aside in favour of keeping the established practices - the traditions - of religious institutions.

To the Jews then, Jesus gave the example of how they were failing to encourage people to honour their father and mother - which is one of the Bible's basic commands, being found among the Ten Commandments (Exodus 20). They were encouraging people to break this command by a misplaced show of piety. Instead of giving a supporting financial contribution to their parents, who were perhaps now elderly and dependent on them, their sons were being taught that it was okay, or even preferable, to say that their funds were dedicated to God, and so couldn't be made available to their parents. This was rank hypocrisy, which probably benefited both themselves and the religious institution at that time.

They dodged this command of God, and thought they were dodging the penalty for dishonouring one's father or mother by using the word "Corban," as Mark calls it (Mark 7:11). All someone had to do to evade duty to father or mother was to say, "Corban," or "Gift," all the time hiding behind the idea of using the money for God. The picture is of a son avoiding his obligation to assist needy parents by uttering the formula: "Whatever that may be by which you might be helped by me, is not mine to give. It is vowed to God." The man, however, wasn't bound to actually give his gift to the temple-treasury because the phrase didn't necessarily go so far as to dedicate the gift to the temple.

By this 'magic' word, as it were, a son who so wished set himself free from obedience to the fifth commandment. Sometimes these disloyal sons even paid the religious leaders for such dodges. It might even have been the case that some of these critics here were guilty of receiving some of the proceeds! But the verse I want you to particularly notice is verse 6; we'll read it again, now that we've explained its context. It says this: "... by this you invalidated the word of God for the sake of your tradition." The word translated as 'invalidated' ('Ekurosate' / 'akuros') means to deprive something of its authority and power, or to render it null and void. This is what these religious legalists were doing with God's Word. The idea in the word means to neutralize the moral force and power of the scriptures, and a common way of doing that is by splitting hairs over technicalities.

And this is exactly what these Jews were doing. You remember their initial criticism of Jesus' disciples had been concerning the fact that Jesus' disciples didn't follow the excessive and superstitious rituals about the washing of hands as elaborated in the Jewish traditions of the time. The Gospel writer, Mark, adds in his record of this same event that this custom of washing extended not merely to their hands before eating, but it also came into play in coming from the market; and also extended to cups, and pots, and brass vessels, and even tables (Mark 7:3,4). They claimed they did this for the sake of cleanliness. That might have been all right, as far as it went. But they also made it a matter of superstition. They regarded external purity as of much more importance than purity of heart. They'd many foolish rules about the exact amount of water that was to be used, the way in which it should be applied, the number of times it should be changed, the number of those that might wash at a time, and all that sort of thing. This shows how they had invalidated God's Word or, in other words, how they had denied the moral force of the Word.

By all these hair-splitting technicalities - which were, of course, of their own making - they had rendered God's Word null and void and powerless in that they had come to regard outward, physical cleanliness as of more importance than moral cleanliness of the heart. We mentioned how this tendency to honour tradition above the pure Word of God has been a besetting sin of religious history, and an extreme example - not totally dissimilar to what we've been reading about in Matthew 15 - once took place in England. It was, for a while, the practice of religious leaders to urge people to make deathbed grants of their land to the established church of the day.

A typical grant would read: "For my salvation, and for the salvation of my predecessors, and for the salvation of my successors, and for the salvation of my wife ... I give and bequeath to God and his Church ... [my land]." Clearly, this evil practice put deathbed grants of land in the place that can only properly be occupied by Jesus Christ, and so, in the most blatant and wicked way, it invalidated the clear word of God regarding the salvation of the soul – that it is by God's grace through faith, and that in Jesus Christ alone (Ephesians 2:8,9). The point is, no matter how devoted we are, it can only be safe for us to consider if there's anywhere at all in our life where we're avoiding the power of God's Word - maybe by some means or other of rationalizing the Bible text or over-ruling its plain meaning by appeal to some other source of authority.

This, after all, is one of the main distinguishing features of a cult - namely that it elevates some other authority to at least the same level as the Bible. We have been warned!

# CHAPTER EIGHT: NEGLECT GOD'S WORD

Years ago an old man living in New Jersey discovered about $5,000 in a family Bible: quite a large sum at that time. The bank notes were scattered throughout the Bible, tucked away in its pages. What had happened was this: in 1874, the man's aunt had died, and part of her will read as follows: "To my beloved nephew, Steven Marsh, I will and bequeath my family Bible, and all it contains, with the residue of my estate after my funeral expenses and just and lawful debts are paid." The estate amounted to a few hundred dollars, which were soon spent. Thereafter, and for about thirty-five years, his chief support had been a small pension from the Government. So he lived in poverty, and yet all the time, within his reach, there was the precious Bible containing thousands of dollars, sufficient for all his wants.

He must have passed by the Bible many times, on a daily basis more than likely. His eyes rested on it, perhaps his hands handled the old leather-bound Bible, with its brass clasps, but he didn't once open it. At last, while packing his trunk, to move finally to live with his son, where he intended to spend his few remaining years, he discovered the unknown riches which had always been in his possession. What thoughts of regret must have come to his mind! If he'd only opened that Bible years earlier, he could have used the money to great advantage! Instead, the treasure lay idle for thirty-five years, during which time he could have been enjoying it to the full!

A sad story. But there's something infinitely sadder than the experience of this man. It's neglect of the Bible itself. God has given us a valuable treasure in his Word. In this Book of books, the power and the riches of the wisdom, knowledge, love and grace of God are all made known in fullest measure. All our spiritual needs can be met through its pages. And yet these riches, put at our disposal by a loving Father, are often unknown and unused riches, are they not? Instead of being enjoyed, they are so often neglected. God's power in our lives as we serve him comes through prayer as we saw in the first chapter; but it also comes through the Word, by which I mean the Bible, God's Word. Few places make that clearer than the way in which the Bible book of Joshua begins, which we should now take the time to read:

> "Now it came about after the death of Moses the servant of the LORD, that the LORD spoke to Joshua the son of Nun, Moses' servant, saying, "Moses My servant is dead; now therefore arise, cross this Jordan, you and all this people, to the land which I am giving to them, to the sons of Israel ... No man will be able to stand before you all the days of your life. Just as I have been with Moses, I will be with you; I will not fail you or forsake you. Be strong and courageous, for you shall give this people possession of the land which I swore to their fathers to give them. Only be strong and very courageous; be careful to do according to all the law which Moses My servant commanded you; do not turn from it to the right or to the left, so that you may have success wherever you go.

This book of the law shall not depart from your mouth, but you shall meditate on it day and night, so that you may be careful to do according to all that is written in it; for then you will make your way prosperous, and then you will have success. Have I not commanded you? Be strong and courageous! Do not tremble or be dismayed, for the LORD your God is with you wherever you go" (Joshua 1:1-9).

To take over the leadership of the people of God after Moses was no small task. There would have been times when it had all but drained Moses of strength. But God who gives us our tasks is an empowering God. The resources of strength and courage so vital to Joshua's mission were shown here to be closely connected to the role of God's Word in the life of God's servant. And this reality has never changed down through all the centuries, although the mission has. The apostle Paul prayed that certain Christians would be strengthened with power (Colossians 1:11). That power is absolutely vital for weathering the storms of life; and for increasing our productivity for God; for enjoying spiritual health and vitality; and spiritual success! But in practical reality, how is this power conveyed to us? Let's turn to Psalm 1:

> "How blessed is the man who does not walk in the counsel of the wicked, nor stand in the path of sinners, nor sit in the seat of scoffers! But his delight is in the law of the LORD, and in His law he meditates day and night. He will be like a tree firmly planted

by streams of water, which yields its fruit in its season and its leaf does not wither; and in whatever he does, he prospers" (Psalm 1:1-3).

Clearly then, we're back once again to prayerfully reading the Bible. Meditating on it is the source of all the power we need. The person who makes it his or her habit to meditate on God's Word will have spiritual stability (the firmness of a tree), spiritual productivity (seasons of fruit), spiritual vitality (leaves that don't wither) and spiritual prosperity (in whatever he or she does). At the root of all these is a daily Bible-reading habit! By contrast, it follows that power will be lost through neglect of God's Word. The apostles, in the earliest days of Christianity, appreciated this fact, as we read in Acts chapter 6:

> "Now at this time while the disciples were increasing in number, a complaint arose on the part of the Hellenistic Jews against the native Hebrews, because their widows were being overlooked in the daily serving of food. So the twelve summoned the congregation of the disciples and said, "It is not desirable for us to neglect the word of God in order to serve tables. Therefore, brethren, select from among you seven men of good reputation, full of the Spirit and of wisdom, whom we may put in charge of this task. But we will devote ourselves to prayer and to the ministry of the word" (Acts 6:1-4).

It's the apostles' words in verse 2 which claim our attention: "It is not desirable for us to neglect the word of God in order to serve tables." The word translated as 'neglect'

('Kataleipsantas'/'kataleipo') basically means to leave behind. I'm sure we've all known times when the demands being placed upon us bring about a measure of withdrawal from Bible meditation and study, and perhaps from preaching too. They were sensitive to the danger of neglecting God's Word. They made prayer and time with their Bibles a priority.

When we do otherwise, we lose spiritual power in our lives. We must meditate daily, prayerfully, profoundly upon the Word if we're to maintain power. Many a person has run dry through its neglect; whereas others have known the power that comes through the regular, thoughtful, prayerful, protracted meditation on God's Word. But then gradually business, and perhaps Christian duties, has multiplied, or other studies have come in, and the Word has, in measure, been crowded out, and so the previous power has gone.

The Lord spoke of this in his famous parable of the Sower in which different types of hearers are like the different types of ground on which the same good seed falls:

> "Behold, the sower went out to sow; and as he sowed, some seeds fell beside the road, and the birds came and ate them up. Others fell on the rocky places, where they did not have much soil; and immediately they sprang up, because they had no depth of soil. But when the sun had risen, they were scorched; and because they had no root, they withered away. Others fell among the thorns, and the thorns came up and

choked them out. And others fell on the good soil and yielded a crop, some a hundredfold, some sixty, and some thirty" (Matthew 13:3-8).

He went on to make totally clear for his disciples - and us - the meaning of that parable when he said:

> "When anyone hears the word of the kingdom and does not understand it, the evil one comes and snatches away what has been sown in his heart. This is the one on whom seed was sown beside the road. The one on whom seed was sown on the rocky places, this is the man who hears the word and immediately receives it with joy; yet he has no firm root in himself, but is only temporary, and when affliction or persecution arises because of the word, immediately he falls away. And the one on whom seed was sown among the thorns, this is the man who hears the word, and the worry of the world and the deceitfulness of wealth choke the word, and it becomes unfruitful. And the one on whom seed was sown on the good soil, this is the man who hears the word and understands it; who indeed bears fruit and brings forth, some a hundredfold, some sixty, and some thirty" (Matthew 13:19-23).

The most relevant part to us is the imagery of the thorny ground. The situation there depicts the man who hears God's Word, but then later the worry of the world, and the deceitfulness of wealth squeeze out any time and place for God's Word in the believer's life. Mark, in his retelling, expands slightly, when he says: "But the worries of the world, and the deceitfulness of riches, and the desires for other things enter in and choke the word, and it becomes unfruitful." (Mark 4:19)

The desires for other things - what a lot this covers! How it challenges our hearts before God. Desires for other things, and attention paid to these things, all add up to neglect of God's Word in our lives - a situation which can only leave us spiritually impoverished. How different was the attitude of the psalmist in Psalm 119, although the way he expresses his desires for God's Word makes it quite clear that he knew the same struggles that we do. His prayer is:

> "Teach me, O LORD, the way of Your statutes and I shall observe it to the end. Give me understanding that I may observe Your law and keep it with all my heart. Make me walk in the path of Your commandments for I delight in it. Incline my heart to Your testimonies and not to dishonest gain. Turn away my eyes from looking at vanity and revive me in Your ways. Establish Your word to Your servant as that which produces reverence for You" (Psalm 119:33-38).

So thankfully, the Psalmist who knew times of spiritual weakness, was also aware of the remedy: which was the Word of God. The same point is made in Psalm 19:

> "The law of the LORD is perfect, restoring the soul;
> The testimony of the LORD is sure, making wise the simple. The precepts of the LORD are right, rejoicing

the heart; The commandment of the LORD is pure, enlightening the eyes. The fear of the LORD is clean, enduring forever; The judgments of the LORD are true; they are righteous altogether" (Psalm 19:7-9).

Did you get that? Are you feeling down, or wearied, feeling a certain powerlessness? His prayer is so relevant to us all in this modern world, with all its pressures. Perhaps you sometimes feel there's not enough time to read everything that pours through your letterbox or into your e-mail inbox? We're living in days of information overload, aren't we? It's the Word of God that can restore our souls! And give us wisdom for those daunting tasks; guidance in those difficult decisions; and the enduring power to do what's right in God's eyes. May God help us to be wise, like the apostles in Acts chapter 6, in finding ways to cut down on all that we've got to look at, so that we don't mistreat God's Word by neglecting it. Let's make sure that our crowded lives don't choke out time spent with God around his Word, the Bible, for neglecting God's Word will without fail stunt our spiritual growth and rob us of spiritual power.

Thomas Aquinas is credited with the words: "hominem unius libri timeo' - meaning "I fear the man of a single book". The sense being, I believe, that it was unwise to trust a man who was very narrow in his education, and who was not a widely read man. But Aquinas' phrase was turned on its head by John Wesley who said '... At any price, give me the Book of God ... here is knowledge enough for me. Let me be homo unius libri!' In other words, his prayer was: 'Lord, make me a man of one book!' From the year 1730, apparently, he largely confined himself to the Bible. And with what results! It's been said that from the unlikely soil [of

England] a grossly immoral, drink-sodden nation of brutalized gamblers on the verge of collapse into absolute infidelity, [there] sprang under God and through Wesley, the evangelical revival of the 18th century, which doubtless spared England a revolution such as befell the French.

Such was the impact, under God, of one man captivated by the Bible, and by the power of the Word. The Lord spoke in the same breath of the Scriptures – the Bible – and the power of God when he answered the Sadducees saying, "You are wrong, because you know neither the Scriptures nor the power of God" (Matthew 22:29 ESV). And he couldn't have been more emphatic about the role the Bible should play in daily Christian living when he said, "Man shall not live by bread alone, but by every word that comes from the mouth of God" (Matthew 4:4 ESV, Deuteronomy 8:3). Our growth and development as Christians is dependent on it, as Paul told the Colossians: "This you have heard before in the word of the truth, the gospel ... which has come to you, as indeed in the whole world it is bearing fruit and growing – as it also does among you, since the day you heard it and understood the grace of God in truth" (Colossians 1:6).

And again in the third chapter, he explained how it's the indwelling word of Christ which teaches and corrects us: "Let the word of Christ dwell in you richly, teaching and admonishing one another in all wisdom, singing psalms and hymns and spiritual songs, with thankfulness in your hearts to God" (Colossians 3:16 ESV). Finally, the full range of the powerful effect of God's Word upon us is described in Paul's last letter to Timothy: "All Scripture is inspired by God and profitable for teaching, for reproof, for correction, for training in righteousness; so that the man of God may be adequate, equipped for every good work" (2 Timothy 3:16-17).

In order to be empowered to do good work for God, there's no substitute for Bible reading and study. If we neglect it, we'll be so much weaker as a result.

# CHAPTER NINE: PEDDLE GOD'S WORD

Have you ever bought something on eBay that turned out to be a con? Or have you perhaps had no end of hassle when buying a second-hand car? The charming salesperson for whom nothing seemed to be too much trouble when you were at the stage of showing interest, suddenly seems to turn into an evasive and unhelpful individual whenever you make the first legitimate complaint. Of course, not all purchasing experiences are like this. There are many professional and courteous dealers with whom it's a pleasure to do business! In some parts of the world today, street-peddlers are still common-place, or people who peddle their wares from house to house. You're much less likely to be able to find them again when you later discover some defect with your purchase. But it was a way of trading that was very common in the ancient world.

Let me ask you, have you ever bought a bag of fruit or vegetables after being attracted to the beautiful produce that was visible through the clear packaging, only to be disappointed when you get home, open the bag and then find that quite a few pieces of fruit hidden away at the centre of the bag are bad? Wasn't it a good idea for the seller not to have placed the bad fruit where they could be seen?! Tricks like that - tricks of the trade - must be as old as human history itself. Some Bible writers drew on their knowledge of this type of practice, and used it to illustrate the work of false teachers: those who were mistreating God's Word. Our example is taken from the New Testament, from the writings of the apostle Paul to the Church of God at Corinth, found in his second Bible letter to them, at the end of the second chapter:

> "But thanks be to God, who always leads us in triumph in Christ, and manifests through us the sweet aroma of the knowledge of Him in every place. For we are a fragrance of Christ to God among those who are being saved and among those who are perishing; to the one an aroma from death to death, to the other an aroma from life to life. And who is adequate for these things? For we are not like many, peddling the word of God, but as from sincerity, but as from God, we speak in Christ in the sight of God (2 Corinthians 2:14-17).

It's that last verse that I'd like to focus on - where Paul says: "For we are not like many, peddling the word of God, but as from sincerity, but as from God, we speak in Christ in the sight of God." In Paul's time, there were those whom he accuses of 'peddling the Word of God'. The word ('Kapeleuo'/ 'kapeleuontes') usually had a different, an everyday kind of use in those days. It normally referred to notorious wine retailers in the markets or to hucksters putting good fruit on top of the basket, giving the impression it was good all the way down to the bottom of the basket, whereas in reality that was far from the case. There's really only one word for traders like that: corrupt. So we find that this word for peddling which Paul uses can equally be translated as corrupting the Word of God. Although this is the only place in the Bible where we find this word, it was, nevertheless, a common word in all stages of Greek, which just goes to show how persistent this kind of fraudulent trading was in everyday life.

The typical kind of dodgy dealer it related to was regarded as a breed apart from those who were described then - by the likes of the Roman writer Plato - as merchants or wholesale dealers. They, by way of contrast, were at the respectable end of the business.

The word whose background we're digging into here included in its scope dealers in victuals and all sorts of wares, but it was especially applied to retailers of wine, with whom adulteration and short measure were matters of course. One writer (Galen) speaks of these wine-dealers playing tricks with their wines; mixing the new, harsh wines, so as to make them pass for old. Another favourite trick, of course, was the old one of diluting or watering down the wine.

These corrupt wine-dealers of the ancient world not only sold their wares in the market, but had wine shops all over the town, where it was not thought respectable to take refreshments. The whole trade was greatly despised. In fact, so widespread was this corrupt trade, that in Thebes no one who had sold in the market within the last ten years was allowed to take part in government. Plato again wrote that if a city wanted to be respectable, it must - he said - have as few of these retail traders as possible ('Laws', 919). This shows how big a problem it was recognized as being.

Paul here uses the term of those who trade in the word of God, adulterating it for the purpose of personal gain or popularity, diluting it perhaps with human philosophy. Sadly, we still have people like that with us today. Outwardly there is a show of piety, but later reports surface that they have been lining their own pockets. And it happens all over the world: in poor countries as well as rich ones. Those who preach God's Word are not always all that they present themselves outwardly as being. They don't withstand the scrutiny of closer inspection. They are well compared to the huckster who puts the good fruit on top of the basket, for they trade in the Word to gain popularity and for self-advantage.

That's a terrible abuse of God's Word - one for which God will bring them into judgement. By their actions many are caused to stumble, and the enemies of God are given opportunity to blaspheme. What they're doing is short-changing others of the fragrance of Christ. In contrast to this despicable behaviour, Paul sets out the example of himself and his companions: "For we are not like many, peddling the word of God, but as from sincerity, but as from God, we speak in Christ in the sight of God" (2 Corinthians 2:17). The apostle stresses his sincerity, the preacher of the Gospel must be sincere. He emphasizes that his message is from God; he was sincerely speaking the message that had been delivered to him to speak by the Lord himself. His preaching is in Christ, he says, and in the sight of God. Paul was always conscious of God's eye upon him as he handled the precious truths of God's Word.

# POWER OUTAGE - CHRISTIANITY UNPLUGGED

Let's continue now with this more positive note, with a comment on the verses which come just before our key text. Let's look at them once again in 2 Corinthians chapter 2: "But thanks be to God, who always leads us in triumph in Christ, and manifests through us the sweet aroma of the knowledge of Him in every place. For we are a fragrance of Christ to God among those who are being saved and among those who are perishing; to the one an aroma from death to death, to the other an aroma from life to life. And who is adequate for these things?" (vv.14-16).

The image is taken from the triumphal procession of a victorious general. A triumph, among the Romans, was a public honour given to a victorious general which took the form of a magnificent procession through the city. The general would usually be dressed in a rich purple robe, and musicians would head up the procession. There would also be a display of carts loaded with the spoils captured from the enemy: horses, chariots, kings, princes, or generals taken in the war, now in chains. During this time all the temples were opened, and every altar smoked with offerings and incense.

Applying all this to himself, Paul regarded himself as a trophy of God's grace, a trophy of God's victorious power in Christ. His almighty conqueror was leading him about, through all the cities of the Greek and Roman world, as an example of the power of God to subdue and to save. Someone has said, "Our only true triumphs are God's triumphs over us". But what distinguishes God's triumph from that of a human general, is that the captive is brought into willing obedience (2 Corinthians 10:5) to Christ, and so joins in the triumph: God 'leads him in triumph' not merely as someone who has been triumphed over, but also as someone triumphing over God's foes with God. As the smoke of the victims and incense offered on such an occasion would fill the whole city with their perfume, so the odour of the name and teaching of Christ filled the whole of Corinth. What a blessing it is when God's Word is handled well!

# CHAPTER TEN: ADULTERATE GOD'S WORD

Perhaps you've heard the story of the country preacher looking for a job. The selection committee ask him, "Do you know much about the Bible?"

"Oh, yes, I know the Bible through and through."

"What's your favourite book?"

"The Gospel by Mark."

"Which part?"

"The Parables."

"Which parable?"

"The parable of the Good Samaritan."

"Can you tell it to the committee?"

He says, "Yes. It goes this way. Once there was this man travelling from Jerusalem to Jericho and he fell among the thorns and the thorns sprang up and choked him. And as he went on he didn't have any money and he met the Queen of Sheba and she gave him a 1000 talents of gold and a 1000 changes of [clothes] and he got into a chariot and drove furiously and when he was driving under a big juniper tree his hair caught on the limbs of that tree and he hung there many days and the ravens brought him food to eat and water to drink and he ate 5000 loaves and 2 fish. One night when he was hanging there asleep, his wife

Delilah came along and cut off his hair and he dropped and fell on stony ground, but he got up and went on and it began to rain and it rained 40 days and 40 nights and he hid himself in a cave and he lived on locusts and honey. Then he went on until he met a servant who said, "Come, let's have supper together," but he made an excuse saying, "No, I can't. I've married a wife and I can't go," and the servant went out to the highways and hedges and compelled him to come in and after supper he went on and came down to Jericho.

When he got there he looked up and saw that old queen Jezebel sitting down high up on the window and she laughed at him and so he said, "Throw her down," and they threw her down, and he said "Throw her down again," and they threw her down 70 times 7 and of the fragments that remained they picked up 12 baskets full besides women and children. And they say, 'Blessed are the piece-makers'. Now whose wife do you think she will be in that judgement day?"

Quite a distortion, isn't it? Sadly, verses are often taken out of context, as the Word of God is distorted to lure people into a commitment. But we dare not preach a forked message. We must never distort the Word of God. That's the kind of thing Paul was speaking against at the beginning of Second Corinthians chapter 4:

> "Therefore, since we have this ministry, as we received mercy, we do not lose heart, but we have renounced the things hidden because of shame, not walking in craftiness or adulterating the word of God, but by

the manifestation of truth commending ourselves to every man's conscience in the sight of God" (2 Corinthians 4:1,2).

Notice how Paul sets himself apart from those who are 'adulterating the word of God'. The basic idea behind the word ('Dolountes'/'doloo'/delo') is 'to catch with bait'. Paul is saying that we cannot use deceptive means. James Fenimore Cooper, a demagogue, says, 'a demagogue is one who advances his own interests by affecting or pretending a devotion to the interests of people. Of all the demagogues, the religious ones are the most despicable - they know how to bait the hook.' Baiting the hook, handling God's Word deceitfully, is the opposite of manifesting the truth. Paul says, we're to hold such a view of the truth as to discard every artful device in public and private. Paul's word here for 'adulterating' is another word which is only found once in the New Testament. Primarily, it means 'to ensnare'; with the additional sense of 'to corrupt'.

It was used within the society of those times to describe the adulteration of the likes of gold and wine. So it has a similar meaning to the last word we studied in Second Corinthians chapter 2, but this one has a narrower meaning than the one used there. While this one also can mean 'to corrupt', there's no thought of doing it for the sake of financial gain here. Let's look at the broader context of Paul's words for there are many interesting things here. He says: "Therefore, since we have this ministry, as we received mercy, we do not lose heart ..."

The danger of losing heart reminds us of those words of James Stewart, that we quoted from his book, 'Heralds of God'. He wrote: 'Surely there are few figures so pitiable as the disillusioned minister of the Gospel. High hopes cheered him on his way, but now the indifference and the recalcitrance of the world, the lack of strikingly visible results, the discovery of appalling pettiness and spite and touchiness and complacency which can lodge in narrow hearts, the feeling of personal futility, all these have seared his soul. 'No longer does the zeal of God's house devour him. No longer does he mount the pulpit steps in thrilled expectancy that Jesus Christ will come amongst his folk that day travelling in the greatness of his strength, mighty to save … The man has lost heart …'

The Apostle Paul, by contrast, wrote, 'we do not lose heart' and then continued: "… but we have renounced the things hidden because of shame, not walking in craftiness or adulterating the word of God, but by the manifestation of truth commending ourselves to every man's conscience in the sight of God." Literally, as we've shown, Paul's saying we're not to use 'bait' in attempting to 'hook' people with the unadulterated Word of God. It's not about impressing anyone, or seeking to gain a following, as Paul now makes clear:

> "For we do not preach ourselves but Christ Jesus as Lord, and ourselves as your bond-servants for Jesus' sake. For God, who said, "Light shall shine out of darkness," is the One who has shone in our hearts to give the Light of the knowledge of the glory of God in the face of Christ. But we have this treasure in earthen vessels, so that the surpassing greatness of the

power will be of God and not from ourselves; we are afflicted in every way, but not crushed; perplexed, but not despairing; persecuted, but not forsaken; struck down, but not destroyed; always carrying about in the body the dying of Jesus, so that the life of Jesus also may be manifested in our body" (2 Corinthians 4:5-10).

Behind these words of Paul, the Old Testament story of Gideon seems to lie in the background. Gideon's story in Judges 7, as you may remember, is an account of how human weakness, with divine help, triumphed. Gideon - still in much fear and trembling - finally overcame overwhelming odds because he was in touch with his God. Gideon's tiny army of only 300 men surrounded the camp of their enemy in the dark of night. Armed with trumpets and torches concealed in clay jars (pitchers), they were granted a miraculous victory by God. At Gideon's signal, the sound of trumpets broke the silence and the clay jars were smashed as light pierced the darkness. That's the picture Paul seems to draw on here, as he describes this world as a dark place spiritually, and goes on to tell us that the battle is on for hearts and minds. Regarding the progress of the Gospel, the imagery here does seem to draw parallels with Gideon's defeat of the Midianites.

Referring to the gospel and its ministry (v.1), Paul says we have it as treasure in jars of clay (v.7). This choice of language, which invites the comparison between treasure and clay, would encourage us to think of our ministry of proclaiming the gospel as much more valuable than life itself. What we possess is as treasure, compared to what we are: mere jars of clay. What's more, these clay jars need to be broken: so that the light of the gospel (v.6); the power that's God's (v.7); and the life of Jesus (v.10) can be seen in this dark world. This is the great positive, and privilege, associated with suffering hardship with the gospel. As you read of these early ministers of the gospel being afflicted, perplexed, persecuted, struck down and always carrying about in the body the dying of Jesus (vv.8-10), picture the breaking of the clay jars. For not only does the truth require to be manifested, but also the life of Jesus (vv.2,11). As a result, our methods will then reflect the message in being wholly without deceit (v.2).

# CHAPTER ELEVEN: WRONGLY DIVIDE GOD'S WORD

The Bible itself, in the New Testament, draws our attention to certain people who handled God's Word crookedly - by departing from the straight and narrow: "... among them are Hymenaeus and Philetus, men who have gone astray from the truth saying that the resurrection has already taken place, and they upset the faith of some" (2 Timothy 2:17-18). These were people who had literally 'swerved away' from the truth of God's Word. They certainly were not handling it in a straightforward way. This way of mistreating God's Word is as old as the human race itself. You can trace its origins to the Garden of Eden, where: "the serpent was more crafty than any beast of the field which the LORD God had made. And he said to the woman, "Indeed, has God said, 'You shall not eat from any tree of the garden?'" (Genesis 3:1).

That was a deliberate bending of the truth, for the question was loaded with the subtle insinuation that God was being repressive in holding back something from our first parents - something which was for their good. Just before we read about the two men who had swerved away from the truth - the two who are named as being like Satan in their behaviour by not handling God's Word of truth in a straightforward way - we read this positive command given to Timothy: "Do your best to present yourself to God as one approved, a workman who does not need to be ashamed and who correctly handles the word of truth" (2 Timothy 2:15 NASB). Or in the words of a different Bible version: "Be diligent to present yourself approved to God, a worker who does not need to be ashamed, rightly dividing the word of truth" (NKJV).

This begins to make even clearer what Hymenaeus and Philetus were doing wrong with the Word of God. They were not rightly dividing it. They were not treating it in an honest and totally straightforward way. They were like people ploughing a furrow that wasn't straight, or perhaps like stone masons who cut their stones in a rough and uneven way because they weren't very skilled at their trade. I remember a time when my wife and I shared a home for a while with another missionary couple. His wife always made out that she needed 'to straighten up the loaf of bread' after I'd finished cutting it.

I'm not entirely convinced that was the case, but some people think there's a background reference here in this word to the task of the household steward as he divided the bread for the household. His task would require him to make straight cuts. You'll get the point, I'm sure, that the basic idea of the word here for accurately handling or rightly dividing God's Word is 'to cut it straight'. Once again in this book we find ourselves studying a word that's only found once in the New Testament. But in the Greek translation of the Old Testament it was used in Proverbs 3:5,6 for making straight paths. You may remember the verses; they are a favourite with many Christians:

> "Trust in the LORD with all your heart
>
> And do not lean on your own understanding.
>
> In all your ways acknowledge Him,

And He will make your paths straight."

That's the very best advice for life. Notice the promise that God will make our paths straight if we trust in him and give him his proper place in our lives. In the New Testament we find that the first disciples - who in all their ways acknowledged Jesus as Lord - were found belonging to what was commonly called in those days, 'the Way'. By allowing God to make their paths straight in his Word, they had been led into God's Way for their lives of service. And the record is left there on the pages of Scripture for us to follow to this day, exactly by making our path straight in God's Word, or, in other words, by rightly dividing God's Word.

I was trying my hand at sea-angling for the first time recently. My companion was a true expert who knew where the fish were, and who patiently showed me the techniques for correctly handling the rod. I enjoyed the experience, and ended up catching the largest fish that day. It brought home to me the advantages of learning a skill from a real expert.

Priscilla and Aquila had that experience when they teamed up with the apostle Paul at the time when:

> "... he left Athens and went to Corinth. And he found a Jew named Aquila, a native of Pontus, having recently come from Italy with his wife Priscilla, because Claudius had commanded all the Jews to leave Rome. He came to them, and because he was of the same trade, he stayed with them and they were

working, for by trade they were tent-makers. And he was reasoning in the synagogue every Sabbath and trying to persuade Jews and Greeks" (Acts 18:1-4).

In fact, I suspect theirs was a double bonus or blessing. I would guess Paul was a competent tent-maker and knew how to cut the rough camel-hair cloth in perfectly straight lines. So perhaps he had some practical tips to pass on to them regarding their tent-making trade? Rightly dividing the material used in tent-making - making straight cuts in the camel-hair cloth - was a basic skill in Paul's day-job. It's very natural then that he should take up this idea and apply it to the main passion of his life, which was handling the Word of God in his preaching.

It's equally true that, as a trained rabbi, Paul would have been very familiar with the Old Testament work of the priests in Israel as they, in a very precise way, butchered the sacrifices: by dividing the animal into its several parts according to the detailed prescriptions found in the Bible book of Leviticus. And, on at least one occasion, Paul spoke of his preaching ministry in these terms. In Romans chapter 15, he says:

> "But I have written very boldly to you on some points so as to remind you again, because of the grace that was given me from God, to be a minister of Christ Jesus to the Gentiles, ministering as a priest the gospel of God, so that my offering of the Gentiles may become acceptable, sanctified by the Holy Spirit" (Romans 15:15-16).

Might it have been that Paul's analogy between his ministry of preaching and the priest's ministry of officiating at the sacrifice extended to the idea of him rightly dividing the Word even as the priests had been charged with rightly dividing the sacrificial victims? Perhaps so, we can't be sure. We'll leave there this important idea of accurately handling the Word of God which, you remember, was in contrast to what those named heretics, Hymenaeus and Phyletus, were doing. They were those who had swerved away from the word of truth. To prevent others, like Timothy, from making that same mistake, Paul encourages us all to: "Be diligent to present yourself approved to God, a worker who does not need to be ashamed, rightly dividing the word of truth" (2 Timothy 2:15 NKJV).

As well as the skilfulness required in the process of rightly dividing the word, it's not hard to see that faithfulness and commitment are also necessary qualities. There's the faithfulness that's involved in being a 'workman'; in other words, someone who toils energetically. In handling God's Word accurately there's no such thing as a short-cut or quick fix. Then there's the degree of commitment which comes across in the instruction to be diligent, to study, to do our best. It demands that we operate at our highest level. If we demand a lot of ourselves in athletic performance or towards career progression or in academic advancement, why should we not exert ourselves to do our very best in the most important field of study of all?

How wrong it is, if Bible study should seem to us to be a matter of low priority. So, as we read, let's observe carefully the context and content of the Bible text, asking - among others - questions like:

- Who was this written to?
- What issue is it addressing?
- How is it expressed in other translations?

Above all, perhaps, we should make John Wesley's prayer our own: "Lord, make me a man of one book!" And what an impact his life had on England - one to which even secular historians have paid tribute. He preached so many sermons in his life (I think it was something like 40,000) all while travelling around the country on horseback - so much so that some feel he gave another meaning to the expression 'the sermon on the mount'! So may the Lord make us men and women of one book: the Bible!

# CHAPTER TWELVE: SUMMING UP

I think the eleven points mentioned – while not exhaustive – probably do give the main ways in which spiritual power is lost. To sum them up they are these: the surrender of our separation, sin, self-indulgence, greed for money, pride, the neglect of prayer, and the various misuses of God's Word. Let's aim, by God's help, from this time on to be on our guard against these things, and to try to make sure of the continuance of God's power in our life and service until the day comes when we can say with Paul: "I have fought the good fight, I have finished the course, I have kept the faith: in the future there is laid up for me the crown of righteousness, which the Lord, the righteous Judge, will award to me on that day" (2 Timothy 4:7-8). We can also, perhaps, make this powerful hymn part of our communion:

O Christ, Thou heavenly Lamb!

Joy of the Father's heart;

Now let Thy love my soul inflame,

Fresh power to me impart.


Power to know the loss

Suffered, O Lord, by Thee;

Power to glory in the Cross

Thou didst endure for me.


Power to feel Thy love,
And all its depths to know;
Power to fix the heart above,
And die to all below.


Power to keep the eye
For ever fixed on Thee;
Power to lift the warning cry
To souls from wrath to flee.


Power lost souls to win
From Satan's mighty hold;
Power the wanderers to bring
Back to the heavenly fold.


Power to watch and pray,
"Lord Jesus, quickly come!"

Power to hail the happy day,

Destined to bear me home.


Lord Jesus, then to me

Power divine impart,

To swell redemption's song to Thee

For worthy, Lord, Thou art.

# Don't miss out!

Visit the website below and you can sign up to receive emails whenever Brian Johnston publishes a new book. There's no charge and no obligation.

https://books2read.com/r/B-A-VLMB-URFW

**BOOKS 2 READ**

Connecting independent readers to independent writers.

Did you love *Power Outage - Christianity Unplugged*? Then you should read *A Test of Commitment: 15 Challenges to Stimulate Your Devotion to Christ* by Brian Johnston!

Bible teacher and radio broadcaster Brian Johnston examines events and objects from the lives of Bible characters to draw out challenging lessons for us as Christians today as to how committed we really are to serve and follow Jesus!

CHAPTER ONE: A GLASS OF WINE (JEREMIAH)

CHAPTER TWO: SCRIBBLING AND SALIVATING AT THE DOORS OF THE GATE (DAVID)

CHAPTER THREE: A VINEYARD IN JEZREEL (NABOTH)

CHAPTER FOUR: A LOVE THAT'S REAL

CHAPTER FIVE: THE PROCEEDS OF A PROPERTY DEAL (ANANIAS AND SAPPHIRA)

CHAPTER SIX: THE SNARE OF THE DEVIL

CHAPTER SEVEN: TEN SILVER COINS AND A SUIT (THE YOUNG LEVITE)

CHAPTER EIGHT: TWO MULES' LOAD OF EARTH (NAAMAN)

CHAPTER NINE: BREAD AND WATER IN THE PROPHET'S HOUSE (JEROBOAM)

CHAPTER TEN: A DIFFERENT KIND OF FIRE (NADAB AND ABIHU)

CHAPTER ELEVEN: A SECOND EPHOD (GIDEON)

CHAPTER TWELVE: A PIECE OF BRASS (HEZEKIAH)

CHAPTER THIRTEEN: SEVEN LOCKS OF HAIR (SAMSON)

CHAPTER FOURTEEN: THE BLEATING OF SHEEP (SAUL)

CHAPTER FIFTEEN: LOVE FOR THE WORLD (DEMAS)

# Also by Brian Johnston

Healthy Churches - God's Bible Blueprint For Growth
Hope for Humanity: God's Fix for a Broken World
First Corinthians: Nothing But Christ Crucified
Bible Answers to Listeners' Questions
Living in God's House: His Design in Action
Christianity 101: Seven Bible Basics
Nights of Old: Bible Stories of God at Work
Daniel Decoded: Deciphering Bible Prophecy
A Test of Commitment: 15 Challenges to Stimulate Your Devotion to Christ
John's Epistles - Certainty in the Face of Change
If Atheism Is True...
8 Amazing Privileges of God's People: A Bible Study of Romans 9:4-5
Learning from Bible Grandparents
Increasing Your Christian Footprint
Christ-centred Faith
Mindfulness That Jesus Endorses
Amazing Grace! Paul's Gospel Message to the Galatians
Abraham: Friend of God
The Future in Bible Prophecy
Unlocking Hebrews
Learning How To Pray - From the Lord's Prayer

About the Bush: The Five Excuses of Moses
The Five Loves of God
Deepening Our Relationship With Christ
Really Good News For Today!
A Legacy of Kings - Israel's Chequered History
Minor Prophets: Major Issues!
The Tabernacle - God's House of Shadows
Tribes and Tribulations - Israel's Predicted Personalities
Once Saved, Always Saved - The Reality of Eternal Security
After God's Own Heart : The Life of David
Jesus: What Does the Bible Really Say?
God: His Glory, His Building, His Son
The Feasts of Jehovah in One Hour
Knowing God - Reflections on Psalm 23
Praying with Paul
Get Real ... Living Every Day as an Authentic Follower of Christ
A Crisis of Identity
Double Vision: Hidden Meanings in the Prophecy of Isaiah
Samson: A Type of Christ
Great Spiritual Movements
Take Your Mark's Gospel
Total Conviction - 4 Things God Wants You To Be Fully Convinced About
Esther: A Date With Destiny
Experiencing God in Ephesians
James - Epistle of Straw?
The Supremacy of Christ
The Visions of Zechariah
Encounters at the Cross
Five Sacred Solos - The Truths That the Reformation Recovered

Kingdom of God: Past, Present or Future?
Overcoming Objections to Christian Faith
Stronger Than the Storm - The Last Words of Jesus
Fencepost Turtles - People Placed by God
Five Woman and a Baby - The Genealogy of Jesus
Pure Milk - Nurturing New Life in Jesus
Jesus: Son Over God's House
Salt and the Sacrifice of Christ
The Glory of God
The Way: Being a New Testament Disciple
Power Outage - Christianity Unplugged
Windows to Faith: Insights for the Inquisitive
Home Truths
60 Minutes to Raise the Dead

# About the Author

Born and educated in Scotland, Brian worked as a government scientist until God called him into full-time Christian ministry on behalf of the Churches of God (www.churchesofgod.info). His voice has been heard on Search For Truth radio broadcasts for over 30 years (visit www.searchfortruth.podbean.com) during which time he has been an itinerant Bible teacher throughout the UK and Canada. His evangelical and missionary work outside the UK is primarily in Belgium and The Philippines. He is married to Rosemary, with a son and daughter.

## About the Publisher

Hayes Press (www.hayespress.org) is a registered charity in the United Kingdom, whose primary mission is to disseminate the Word of God, mainly through literature. It is one of the largest distributors of gospel tracts and leaflets in the United Kingdom, with over 100 titles and hundreds of thousands despatched annually. In addition to paperbacks and eBooks, Hayes Press also publishes Plus Eagles Wings, a fun and educational Bible magazine for children, and Golden Bells, a popular daily Bible reading calendar in wall or desk formats. Also available are over 100 Bibles in many different versions, shapes and sizes, Bible text posters and much more!

www.ingramcontent.com/pod-product-compliance
Lightning Source LLC
Chambersburg PA
CBHW021210020426
42331CB00003B/297